THE
MARKETING
PLAN

THE
MARKETING
PLAN

How to Prepare and Implement It

New, Expanded Edition

William M. Luther

amacom
American Management Association
New York • Atlanta • Boston • Chicago • Kansas City • San Francisco • Washington, D.C.
Brussels • Toronto • Mexico City

This publication is designed to provide accurate and authoritative
information in regard to the subject matter covered. It is sold with
the understanding that the publisher is not engaged in rendering
legal, accounting, or other professional service. If legal advice or
other expert assistance is required, the services of a competent
professional person should be sought.

Library of Congress Cataloging-in-Publication Data

Luther, William M.
        The marketing plan : how to prepare and implement it / William M.
    Luther.—New, expanded ed.
        p.   cm.
    Includes index.
    ISBN 0-8144-7805-0
    1. Marketing. I. Title.
    HF5415.L83   1992   92-17618
    658.8'02—dc20   CIP

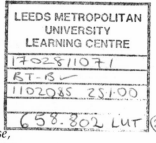

Printing number

12

To
my wonderful wife,
Betty

Contents

Preface

The purpose of this book is to take you through the development of a marketing plan. Not the type of marketing plan that numbers 250 pages. Not one that you write once a year and then put on your shelf for the rest of the year. (Does that sound familiar?) No, this marketing plan, when completed, has fewer than ten pages and is read and approved by management before a penny is ever spent on marketing. It contains measurable objectives so you know whether what you set out to do is accomplished.

The original edition of *The Marketing Plan* was published in 1982. In this new, expanded edition, I have not changed the basic thrust of my message, which is briefly summarized in this preface. However, now that I have benefited from another ten years of consulting, I have made many changes in content in an attempt to clarify my recommendations—and, of course, to reflect changes in the business environment that affect marketing planning.

The completed plan is operational rather than an exercise. It provides specific direction for the five components of marketing: product/service, marketing communications (advertising, sales promotion, and public relations), marketing research, customer service, and sales management. If you don't include all five areas of marketing, you have an incomplete plan; if individuals from these functional areas don't get together and write the plan in unity, poor coordination and improper selection and use of available marketing tools will probably be the result.

As you implement the plan, you may realize that some of

your objectives are too high or too low or that one or more strategies and plans are ineffective. If so, don't wait until the end of the planning year to change your plan; otherwise you lose both time and money.

The marketing plan should become the job descriptions for members of the marketing team. As the plan changes, so do the job descriptions. That means that if you have used the same job descriptions longer than a year, they are probably out of date. In addition, the marketing plan should be the structure for determining the bonuses and advancement for individual members and departments of the marketing team. Those who reach or exceed their measurable objectives should be the only individuals to receive rewards and promotions.

This book will not solve all your marketing problems, but it is hoped that it will give you direction on how to set your objectives and develop your strategies and plans. It appears that most marketing people spend most of their time trying to determine what to do and the few remaining hours on how to execute their decisions. The problem here is that execution is actually the most difficult and time-consuming ingredient. The answer is the development of a tight marketing plan that takes fewer than thirty days to complete, leaving at least 335 days for execution.

The book begins with a chapter on strategic planning, which sets the direction for all subsequent plans, including the marketing plan. There is no way a marketing plan can be written until someone defines the strategic plan. Not only will you probably be out of business in ten years if your company doesn't have a strategic plan, but in the interim, you could be allocating your marketing dollars to the wrong products or services.

I don't expect you to agree with everything in this book. However, the format presented is not unlike the plans prepared today by some of the most successful marketing companies in the country.

William M. Luther
Stamford, Connecticut

Introduction

This book is divided into seven sections. Section I is concerned with the development of the strategic plan and fact book; their relationship to the marketing plan; and the responsibilities of company marketing personnel and advertising agencies as they relate to the preparation and execution of these vital documents.

Sections II through VI are devoted to the five components of marketing. Section VII pulls the five components together with a recommended marketing plan format, including examples of objectives and strategies for each component (see Figure I-1).

Section I begins with strategic planning, with major emphasis on five matrices to help you determine which products and services should receive marketing dollars and which should not. It doesn't do you much good to launch an aggressive marketing program in a market that offers relatively low profit potential or where the competition is much stronger than you are. What you should look for are markets with relatively high profit potential and where you have the resources to become number one or two in market share.

Chapter 2 is devoted to marketing personnel and outlines their tasks and decision areas as well as their relationship to other departments within the company. Chapter 3 discusses how to select an advertising agency, how to work with it, how to get the most out of its services, and how to compensate it.

Chapter 4 covers the fact book, the document that determines the soundness of your marketing plan. If you have an extensive and accurate fact book, you should end up with a

Figure I-1. Schematic of planning process.

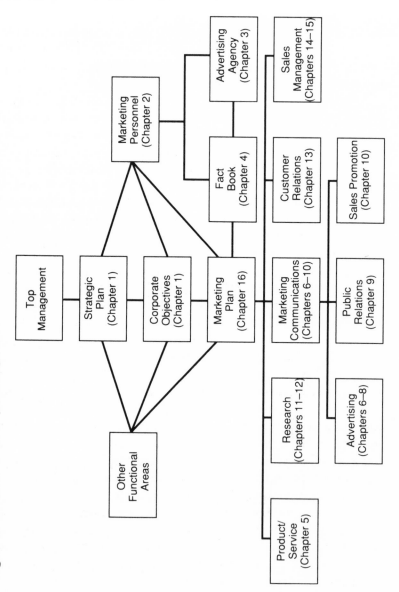

meaningful plan; if your fact book is incomplete and contains a bunch of guesses, you will end up with a lousy plan.

Section II contains Chapter 5 and recommends what information should be in your product/service plan, including pricing strategy; packaging; number of sizes, shapes, and colors; estimated awareness and preference levels; and distribution. A "what if" model helps you look at how these various factors influence each other.

Section III contains five chapters devoted to the development of your marketing communications plan, which includes the advertising plan, public relations plan, and sales promotion plan. The first three chapters are on the advertising plan. Chapter 6 suggests ways to determine what information should be in your basic selling line, Chapter 7 discusses which advertising vehicles you should use to get the story out, and Chapter 8 focuses on how to prepare the message. Chapter 9 discusses one of the most underused marketing tools—public relations—and underlines the many opportunities in this area. Chapter 10 covers the sales promotion plan and explains the advantages and disadvantages of ten different types of sales promotion.

Section IV is devoted to research and contains two chapters. Chapter 11, on market research, discusses how to find the answers to five critical questions: Who are the customers; what do they want; what does the competition offer; what can you offer; and what do customers think you offer? The chapter also discusses how to conduct a benchmark study, including how to establish the correct sample size. Chapter 12, on communications research, offers recommendations on how to determine whether your communications are working.

Section V contains Chapter 13, on customer relations. It costs less than half the marketing dollars to keep a customer than it does to acquire a new one. Then why do so few companies have effective customer relations? Because they don't treat this area as a component of marketing. The impact of this discrepancy is underscored by an examination of well-known companies, including Disney and your local telephone company.

Section VI includes two chapters on the last of the five marketing components covered in this book—sales management. Chapter 14 is devoted to how to manage your sales force and includes my recommended management strategy, referred to as sales management by objectives. Chapter 15 discusses the requirements of an effective sales presentation and discusses thirteen guidelines that should be reviewed by salespeople every single weekday morning.

Section VII is the last section and contains Chapter 16. It ties together the five components of marketing by including a recommended marketing plan format, including examples of objectives, strategies, and plans for each area.

The conclusion summarizes ways to execute the strategies presented in this book.

Section I

Planning and People

1

Strategic Planning

This chapter is not meant to be all-inclusive on the subject of strategic planning. That would take a complete book. The purpose is to convey the importance of strategic planning and to emphasize the fact that all your products and services do not have the same natural strategies. The strategic plan should be completed first, because it sets the direction of the marketing plan.

Planning in a Changing World

The world is in a state of flux, and no one knows for sure what will happen down the road. In the original edition of this book, written in 1982, I stated that by 1990, 25 percent of workers would be operating out of their homes, robots would be everywhere, voice mail would replace switchboard operators, and trees would be used for chemicals rather than for paper. At least I got one out of four; you may be irritated by voice mail if you are the sender, but this technology is here to stay.

Here are some new prognostications. By the year 2000, there will be cures for most types of cancer, and most individuals will live until at least ninety years of age. This will prompt management to realize that "gray heads sell better than blonds" (a possible new book for me), and those companies that are the first to adopt this strategy will have a definite advantage handling the complexities of world markets. And most markets will be worldwide in scope, rather than local. For example, the only automobile manufacturers left on the globe will be General Motors, Ford, Mercedes-Benz, Toyota, and

Honda. All others will not be able to compete because of the economies of scale of those big five automakers.

Computer-aided design (CAD), computer-aided engineering (CAE), computer-aided manufacturing (CAM), and their derivatives will be the rule rather than the exception, resulting in a shrinkage in the life cycle for both products and services from the five- to twenty-year span in the past, to a one- to five-year span in the future. (Some industries are already experiencing this shortened life cycle.) Many people contend that quality is today's single most important product/service ingredient. That may be true, but with such short life cycles, the importance of marketing will not diminish. Rather, it will expand.

And 25 percent of the working population will work out of their homes, robots will be everywhere, and trees will be used for the building blocks of chemicals rather than paper (better late than never).

Will I be right with these prognostications? No one knows for sure. That's the point and the purpose of strategic planning. You look into the future to determine what you believe will happen and then start making plans today to take advantage of the changing conditions. You keep monitoring your predictions for the future, and when or if your vision changes, you alter your plan.

IBM's Strategic Planning

That is not to say that corporations didn't use strategic planning in the past. The former chariman of IBM, Thomas Watson, Jr., said to his management some years back, "We don't want to be in this punch card business all our life. We should get into the computer business. That's where all the action is going to be." At that time, IBM had little or no experience in the computer industry, so Watson decided the company's immediate need was to establish the largest data bank in existence on computers.

Letters went out to all IBM salespeople telling them to immediately send the home office a list of all computers in their territories, including the names of the owner/user companies and their industries; the brand names, model numbers, and ages of the computers; the names of the people who used the computers and the purposes of the use; and in what areas the computers did not perform adequately.

Being typical salespeople, the field staff submitted information on a few computers and then went back to selling punch cards. When Watson realized what was happening, he sent out a second letter, reminding the salespeople that they were frequently transferred and stating that if a new person coming into a territory found one single unreported computer, the previous salesperson would be fired. Within a short period of time, Watson had his research.

IBM compiled the data and determined what computers were serving what industries and the various ages of the equipment. Watson and his people then looked for areas where the competition was not fulfilling the needs of the different industries. After they found the untapped segments, Watson called in his engineers and told them to design computers that would fill the voids.

After the engineers had completed their mission, Watson called together his salespeople to introduce them to the new IBM line of computers. When they returned to the field, not only did they have all the information on the new line of computers, they had day-to-day itineraries on what companies to call on and all the other background information from the extensive data bank.

Across the country, IBM sales personnel went into various companies and said, "Hi, I'm John Smith from IBM. It's my understanding that you have computer XYZ, and it's five years old. It currently handles your payroll but is inadequate for all the other needs you have in this department." Customers were amazed at the extent of IBM's market research, but that's not all that impressed them. Before they could catch their breath, the salespeople displayed the new IBM computers. Not only could the IBM computers do more than anything else on the market, they were substantially less expensive. The rest of the story is history.

What to Avoid

As examples of what happens when a company does not continually look into the future are the financial difficulties faced by Sears and General Motors' Cadillac Division in the early 1990s. Sears either did not have a crystal ball or, if it did, it was so dirty no one could see into it. Sears used to have a unique image, but in recent years it tried to copy everyone from K-mart to Ralph Lauren. Remember the wonderful catalog that was mailed to you? The catalog industry boomed—so Sears de-emphasized its catalog business. Today you have to go to a store to see a catalog, and there are so many editions that you never know where to look. J. C. Penny has effectively taken the lucrative catalog business away from Sears.

What does the typical Cadillac owner want in a car? Size. What did Cadillac do? It downsized to make its autos look like all the rest of the smaller models. The brand then lost one-third of its market share. Conversely, what did Buick do? It continued to offer what its customers wanted: old-style V-8, rear-wheel-drive cars with vintage names like Roadmaster, Park Avenue, and Regal. As of this writing, within General Motors, Buick sales are now second only to Chevrolet, and gaining. And it appears that the designers, engineers, and marketing personnel within the Cadillac group that work on the Cadillac Seville paid more attention to what the customer wanted than their peers did. They increased the size of this model, improved the quality, and gave it distinctive lines. Today, the Seville is ranked by many as an equal to the Japanese Infiniti and Lexus.

What Strategic Planning Is Not

Before getting into the key elements of strategic planning, it may be helpful, because there is so much confusion on the subject, to first state what strategic planning is not. It is not the application of a scientific method. There is no set formula. It is less a technique than a responsibility. It is more than forecasting, which is basically projecting the past into the future. It is not making decisions in the future; the only time you can make a decision is in the present.

What Strategic Planning Is

Then what is strategic planning? It is a commitment by management to look into the future of markets to determine which products or services should be aggressively promoted, which ones maintained, and which ones abandoned; to decide which businesses should be acquired and which sold; and to establish priorities in the direction of new product development.

When looking ahead five to ten years, management has to ask many questions and then estimate the probability of each answer becoming a reality. What technological advances are envisioned? What amount of federal and state government regulations will be in force? What direction will competitors take? What business (or businesses) is the corporation in now? What business (or businesses) should the corporation be in five years from now? Ten years? If the corporation were to distribute 100 units of new money, how should it be allocated over the next three, five, and ten years? What should be the optimum location, size, and type of production facilities for the corporation in five years? Ten years?

Since strategic planning should begin with each product/ service line, business unit, or what is referred to as an SBU (strategic business unit), it will be examined first at the unit level and then at the corporate level.

There are four key elements of strategic planning at the SBU level:

1. Identification of the business
2. Situation analysis
3. Selection of strategies
4. Establishment of controls

Identifying the Business

In his article "Marketing Myopia," Theodore Levitt* raises many interesting questions, some of which have precipitated major changes in the way corporations view their businesses. Levitt points out that the reason many corporations got themselves into financial difficulties was not because their markets

*This article appeared in *The Harvard Business Review* in September-October 1975 but has been updated several times since. There have been more requests for reprints of this article than any other that has ever appeared in the magazine.

dried up or new competition appeared. They went bankrupt because they didn't realize what business they were really in. He gives the railroads as one example. Railroads did not get into trouble because there was a decrease in demand for freight or passenger travel; the demand actually increased every year. Nor did they go broke because of the invention of the automobile and the airplane. The railroads' problem was that they thought they were in the railroad business. According to Levitt, they were in the transportation business.

This problem is not uncommon. As previously mentioned, Sears doesn't seem to be able to locate its business. Western Union could never get over the fact that the telegraph was no longer viable.

Alfred Hitchcock, on the other hand, considered himself in the "gooseflesh" business. Minnesota Mining & Manufacturing (3M) says its business is coatings. IBM states that it began in the punch card business, graduated to computers, and is now dealing with the office of the future. AT&T's efforts to redefine itself did not work as well. It spun off its "baby Bell" subsidiaries so that the federal government would let it get into the telecommunications business. AT&T thought its name on a computer would mean something to potential buyers. It didn't.

You are probably beginning to realize that determining what business you are in, or should be in, is not always easy. Look at your various competitors. Try to find one or more that have the same customers as you do; offer similar functions, styles, features, and benefits; and whose strategy affects your own. When you locate such a business, the sum of these activities is the business you are in. If you don't like your grouping, either because you believe your competitors are too strong or because the business doesn't have a future, consider a repositioning. Think it out. Don't pull a Sears, but don't freeze like Western Union.

Situation Analysis

After you decide what business you are in, the next step is the situation analysis. As its title implies, the situation analysis is a review of the current situation for a particular business. This analysis can include market size and growth or decline, technology, regulations, terms and conditions, pricing, distribution, vertical integration, barriers to entry, the strengths and weaknesses of your competitors, and your own strengths and weaknesses. However, be careful here that you don't spend weeks putting together a 250-page analysis of the past. The question to be answered is which brands or products have a future, not what is your overall marketing strategy. That comes later, as detailed in subsequent chapters, and only for brands whose prospects look good.

There are five matrices (see Figure 1-1 through 1-5) to be examined first:

1. Share of market and return on investment
2. Production curve
3. Market life cycle up to middle 1980s
4. Market life cycle for many products/services today
5. Selection of businesses to push

It is a good idea to first obtain the necessary facts and figures you will need to complete the five matrices. Then you can go back and fill in any additional marketing facts that you believe are necessary.

Share of Market and ROI

The first matrix (Figure 1-1) illustrates the relationship between market share and return on investment as reflected in the Profit Impact of Marketing Strategies (PIMS) study. *Market share* is defined as the percentage of the total market or industry accounted for by a business, in either dollars or units. *Return on investment* (ROI) is defined as the ratio between net profit before taxes and the business's total investment in plant and equipment and working capital. The purpose of the PIMS study was to determine whether any of the various business strategies had a direct effect on increasing ROI. With the possible exception of increasing the price of stock, a greater ROI is the number one objective of most companies.

The PIMS methodology originated at General Electric; it

Figure 1-1. Share of market and return on investment matrix. (Courtesy Strategic Planning Institute, Cambridge, Mass.)

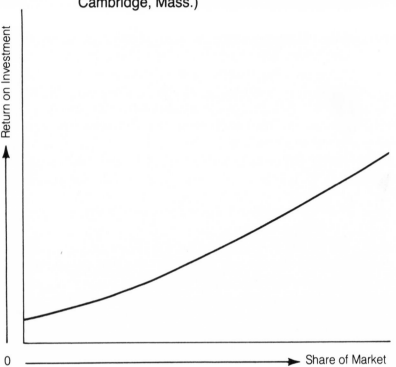

0 ──────────────────────────────► Share of Market

went through the developmental phase at the Harvard Business School and is currently organized as an autonomous nonprofit organization called the Strategic Planning Institute. The ongoing study, begun in 1970, examines corporations participating in over 2,000 businesses. The businesses in the database include consumer product manufacturers, capital equipment manufacturers, raw material producers, components manufacturers, industrial supplies manufacturers, and service and distribution businesses.

The study has indicated that thirty-seven factors tell 80 percent of the ROI story, with market share having the most direct relationship. In fact, the case histories indicated that every 10 percent increase in market share resulted in a 5 percent increase in ROI. For example, if a business was able to increase share from 20 percent to 30 percent, the company could normally expect a 25 percent increase in ROI for that business unit.

Three major reasons are given to explain why market share leads to greater returns. First is economics of scale. The larger the business, the greater the savings in cost of goods, manufacturing, and marketing. Second is market power. A larger company is able to bargain more effectively, even to administer prices, and consequently receives a higher markup. For years, General Motors priced its cars to dealers just above the manufacturing costs of American Motors (eventually acquired by Chrysler). It could have priced them much lower because the economics of scale provided GM with enormous savings in cost of goods. But by pricing them as it did, GM received a much higher markup and could say to the government, "Hey, we're good guys. We're keeping our prices up so AMC can survive." (Alas.) Third is quality of management. Larger companies can attract better managers—managers who are able to increase productivity, decrease costs, and provide overall superior leadership.

Because of the importance of market share, you should include this information on all your products and services in your situation analysis. Today, very few companies cannot obtain at least a close approximation of these statisics. Your sales force can provide information, although you have to be careful that they don't inflate their sales figures. Trade associations, trade publications, and the United States government are other excellent sources. The government should no longer be considered just a body that constantly demands information. There are more data in that labyrinth than in all market research companies combined. The only problem is discovering which department has what you need. You have to be industrious and willing to make several inquiries, but eventually you'll find the right one.

After the government, market research companies can furnish the most accurate and extensive information on market share. Whereas the other sources are usually free, going this direction will cost you money. It may be worth it, however, since market research companies can provide all phases of marketing information for any industry on a national, regional, or individual market basis.

The Production Curve

The share of market and return on investment matrix is closely related to the production curve (Figure 1-2). (A more sophisticated version of this concept is the experience curve, developed by The Boston Consulting Group.) The production curve illustrates that as a business gains greater experience in its field or increases production, it is able to reduce unit costs. On the basis of extensive studies, it was determined that unit costs decline at a fairly constant rate for various industries each time production or experience (number of man-hours) doubles. For example, according to The Boston Consulting Group, each time steel manufacturers were able to double their experience or volume, they cut unit costs approximately 20 percent; for television manufacturers, it was 15 percent, and for the auto industry, 12 percent. Today, computer chips probably have the steepest decline rate of any industry, one in the area of 50 to 70 percent.

The reasons that cost can be reduced as experience or production increases are similar to the reasons for the relationship between the share of market and ROI. Longer production

Figure 1-2. Production curve.

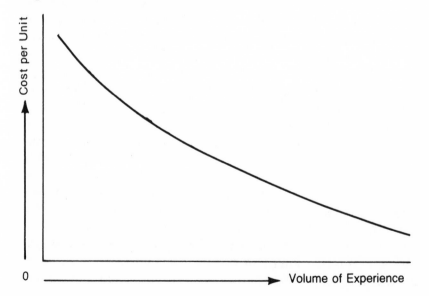

runs, greater managerial experience, standardization of parts, and improved working methods are just a few.

The Japanese appear to understand the production curve much better than most U.S. companies do. It was this concept that helped the Japanese gain such a large market share with their automobiles in the 1960s. (The small size of the cars didn't hurt, either.) The Japanese kept increasing their automobile manufacturing volume in Japan until they obtained a relatively high volume and then established sales organizations in other countries around the world. They selected primarily undeveloped countries, where there was little or no competition. It was not until their production curve had reached a favorable position that they made a major commitment to the U.S. market.

At that time, U.S. automobile production was experiencing only a 3.9 percent increase per year, which on a compounded basis meant it would take eighteen years for the volume to double. This resulted in only a .7 percent annual decline in real costs (12% ÷ 18). The inflation rate in the United States was 4.1 percent, which forced the U.S. automobile producers to increase prices at the rate of 3.4 percent (4.1% − .7%).

The Japanese, however, were increasing their annual volume at an explosive rate of 37 percent. They were able to double their volume every two and one-half years, compared with eighteen years for the U.S. manufacturers. Although the inflation rate was higher in Japan (4.6 percent), Japanese automakers could maintain the same profit without increasing prices.

The Japanese applied the same concept to the motorcycle industry. U.S. manufacturers ceded the low end of the domestic product line to the Japanese because there was relatively little profit in the small machines. The Japanese kept building more and more motorcycles, concentrating on the lightweight, inexpensive models at the beginning and then adding more larger units each year. They kept increasing volume and experience until finally they controlled the entire market. By 1981, only one U.S. motorcycle manufacturer was left.

The Japanese have also used the same marketing strategy with ball bearings. They initially were given the low-cost, low-technology segment of the market. They kept making more and more ball bearings, increasing their technology and expertise, and now they are the dominant source in the world. The Japanese are predominant in steel and shipbuilding, and they practically monopolize the consumer electronics business. They are rapidly becoming more powerful in the computer hardware business and, in a few years, should also be a dominant player in computer software.

If costs are an important factor in your business, you should tabulate your costs today against what your costs were when total accumulative volume was only 50 percent of total accumulative volume to date. Be sure to use real dollars, adjusted for inflation. After you determine the rate or percentage decrease, you can project future savings at that point when it is anticipated that total accumulative volume will double once again.

For example, if your unit costs today are $85 and they were $100 when total accumulative volume was half of total accumulative volume to date, you are on a 85 percent curve. When your total accumulative volume in the future doubles once again, your unit costs should be $72.25 (85 percent of $85). This matrix delivers final approximate costs and is based on the assumption that you will take all economic advantages of increased volume and scale. If possible, you should also make similar cost projections for your competition.

Market Life Cycle

The next matrix that should be examined in the situation analysis describes the market life cycle (Figure 1-3). The market life cycle is usually divided into four segments: introduction, growth, maturity, and decline. It is important to ascertain the life cycle position for your industry because only certain marketing strategies are natural for each stage, regardless of whether the industry is greeting cards or indoor tennis clubs. A natural strategy is one that is relatively easy to achieve. You have favorable market characteristics to go in this direction. The odds are with you. Strategies that go against the grain of the market are considered unnatural. That doesn't mean you can't achieve them, but the odds are against it.

Marketing factors that can help determine what stage a

Figure 1-3. Market life cycle up to the middle 1980s.

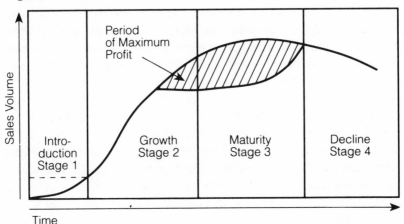

market is in include growth rate, pricing, number of competitors, product modifications, depth of product line, market segmentation, and promotional expenditures.

In the introductory or embryonic stage, which includes test marketing, there is usually only one company manufacturing or providing the new product or service. Surprisingly, it often takes a competitor to push a product out of the introductory stage into the growth period. Just one company cannot normally make sufficient promotional noise to obtain wide acceptance. In the introductory segment, sales are increasing, but not as fast as in the growth stage. Generally, the natural strategy is to price the service high, since the buyer cannot make a direct comparison with another product and determine intrinsic value, and a high price increases the rate of recovery of development costs. Still, there are benefits to the opposing strategy of introducing a product at a low price. A low introductory price can expand the market more rapidly, extend the life of the product, and discourage competition.

Product modifications are frequent during the introductory period, with the manufacturer or service organization trying to eliminate the bugs before the growth stage. Depth of product line is limited, market segmentation is not considered, and unit promotional expenditures are medium to high.

When sales begin to increase rapidly, an industry enters

the growth stage. Many competitors now enter the market to get in on a good thing and force prices down to a competitive level. This is the ideal time for maximum market penetration (increasing market share), supported by very heavy promotional activities. In the early part of this period, product modifications are infrequent because companies are having difficulty just producing all they can sell, but in the latter stages, depth of product lines starts to expand to further increase sales appeal.

After the growth stage comes maturity, when product growth is usually no greater than the growth of the gross national product. Your objective, as a marketing person, should be to keep your product or service from sliding into this stage. Some companies succeed better than others. One of the most successful was Du Pont, with nylon. Nylon was originally conceived for the parachute industry. After the war, demand for parachutes dropped, and nylon would have gone into maturity and decline if Du Pont had not invented new uses. Du Pont looked around and said, "Why not hosiery?" The life cycle line shot straight up again. When the hosiery market started to mature, Du Pont said, "What else? Why not tires?" Once again, the industry life cycle shot upward. When the tire industry matured, Du Pont said, "Why not carpeting?"

Using baking soda as a refrigerator deodorant is another example of finding new uses for products and extending the growth stage of the life cycle. Serving breakfast at McDonald's and home delivery of pizza are other examples of product extensions keeping a market from sliding into maturity.

What these companies have accomplished is not easy. In fact, 75 percent of all business assets in North America are in mature industries. This is the primary reason why so many companies look overseas for future growth. The Ford Motor Company would be close to bankruptcy today if it were not for its highly successful European operation. Even the Coca-Cola Company receives 80 percent of its profit from outside the United States.

The major problem with industries in the mature stage is that there are not many natural marketing strategies available. Market penetration is an unnatural strategy, not only because it is extremely difficult to accomplish but because it is extremely expensive. This is not to say it can't be done. One example is Miller Beer, which competes in the mature beer industry. When Philip Morris bought Miller Brewing Company in 1970, Miller Beer was in sixth place with a 3.4 percent market share. In 1979 it was second only to Anheuser-Busch, with a 24.5 percent share. Their unnatural strategy succeeded, but a corporation without the financial resources of a Philip Morris probably would have failed. Wal-Mart and Woolworth (that's right, Woolworth, which owns Foot-Locker and Lady Foot-Locker) are other examples of companies that have been able to gain share in mature markets.

Another advantage Philip Morris had up until 1978 was that Anheuser-Busch did not fight back. However, in 1979, young Augie Busch took control of the company and proceeded to launch an aggressive attack against Miller Brewing Company. He doubled the marketing budget and began to dominate special events advertising in events like rodeos and stock car and speedboat racing. He introduced several new brands like Bud Light, Bud Dry, and Michelob Light. Today Anheuser-Busch has a market share of 44 percent versus 18 percent for Miller Brewing Company.

The most natural strategy in a mature industry is cost efficiency. Your primary objective should be the development of new technology and human resources procedures that lower operating costs. Vertical integration, both upward and downward, is considered a natural strategy in the latter part of the growth period and into the mature stage since it is a means to cut costs. If you were a paper manufacturer, the only justification for purchasing forests would be cost efficiency. If you were in the introductory or early stages of the growth period, vertical integration would be an unnatural, and possibly dangerous, strategy. Not only would you need all your financial resources to promote the brand, but if the industry were to fail, you certainly wouldn't want to be caught with a huge investment.

The purpose of cost efficiency in the mature stage is that it enables you to cut, or at least maintain, prices in an attempt to force out the smaller and less efficient competitors. If the industry is in a low-growth or nongrowth stage and you eliminate all or most of the competition, you can still remain profitable, even with a smaller margin, by taking a bigger slice of the market. Market segmentation and annual product modifications, or planned obsolescence, such as practiced by the automobile industry, are also natural strategies in the mature stage.

In the decline or aging segment of the life cycle, growth is less than the growth of the gross national product. Here there are even fewer natural strategies than in the mature stage. Usually only one or two competitors are left in the market, and there is little or no promotional activity.

There are no specific time periods to any of the four stages of the life cycle. The computer business has been in the growth stage for forty years. The stages are also reversible. The bicycle industry was in the mature stage in the 1960s and early 1970s. Then in 1976 it reentered the growth stage; as many bicycles were sold as cars. And in 1979, 12 million bicycles were sold, compared with only 8 million automobiles. All stages of the industry life cycle can be profitable, but it is important to remember that the same basic strategies apply to practically all industries when they are in the same stage of the life cycle.

Since the middle 1980s, the market life cycle has changed dramatically for some industries, as shown in Figure 1-4. No longer do companies in many industries, especially high tech-

Figure 1-4. Market life cycle in the 1990s.

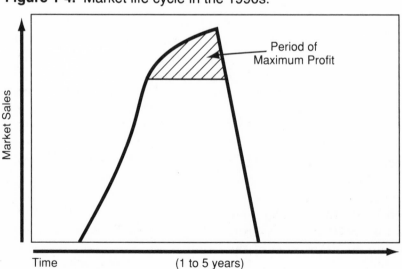

nology, enjoy the long period of maximum profit shown in Figure 1-3. It used to be that you could get good financial returns during the later part of the growth cycle and during the early maturity cycle. Today that is not always true; there may not even be an early maturity stage if the product or service is replaced by new technology before it gets to that stage of the life cycle.

Neither the original Apple personal computer nor the IBM PC ever reached maturity; both were replaced by machines twenty times faster than they were before they could get to that stage. Advances in computer technology came rapidly; Compaq came out with portable computers, Apple's Macintosh offered superb graphics, and Microsoft's Windows software extended this graphics capability to other personal computers. Sun Microsystems cornered a huge slice of the market with its workstations, and the Japanese scored a major advance with laptop computers. No wonder John Young, CEO of Hewlett-Packard, stated that one of most critical strengths of a business is time to market.

Selection of Businesses to Push

This is the last and most inclusive of the matrices presented in this book that you can use in your situation analysis to help determine your strategies. Figure 1-5 incorporates what I consider the three most important overall factors that influence whether you will make money in a market: the profit potential of the market, competitor strengths, and your company's strengths. Profit potential means the degree of profitability of a market if you have or can acquire the critical strengths needed to become number one or two in market share. Competitor strengths means the degree of critical strengths your competitors possess or can acquire. Your company's strengths refers to the same critical strengths, but for your own company. Figure 1-5 presents eight typical business situations. They are:

1. An existing market with high profit potential in which you have the required critical strengths and your competition does not

2. A new market with high profit potential in which nei-

Figure 1-5. Selection of businesses to push (one offering the greatest opportunity, eight the least).

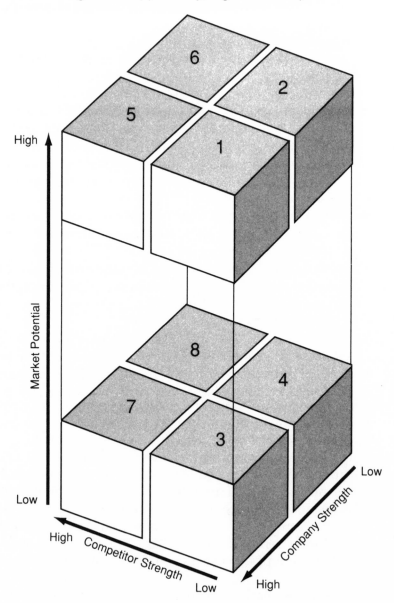

ther you nor your competition have yet acquired the necessary critical strengths

3. An existing market with relatively low profit potential in which you have the required critical strengths but your competition does not
4. A new market with relatively low profit potential in which neither you nor your competition has yet acquired the necessary critical strengths
5. An existing market with high profit potential in which both you and competition have the required critical strengths
6. An existing market with high profit potential in which you do not have the required critical strengths but your competition does
7. An existing market with relatively low profit potential in which both you and your competition have the required critical strengths
8. An existing market with relatively low profit potential in which you do not have the required critical strengths but your competition does

Placing each of your businesses in the appropriate cube or market can help you select which businesses should be pushed, which maintained, and which phased out. A business is defined as one or more products/services that you sell to one set of customers. Let's take one cube at a time.

Cube 1,

a business situation in which the market offers excellent margins and you either have more resources than your competition has to help you become the strongest or are the market leader. This can be the ideal. The problem is there are very few markets that offer this advantage to just one company; and if one does come along, your competition will soon be closing in on you. Microsoft, a computer software developer, and Intel, a computer microprocessor manufacturer, currently enjoy this situation, and they may have the strength to endure. The CEO of Microsoft, Bill Gates, was a billionaire before the age of thirty and is always appearing on the cover of business magazines.

But such cases are the minority. In fact, some companies will not enter or stay in a hot market because they know the competitive pressure will be great.

Cube 2,

a new market in which the market appears to offer excellent margins but is too young for any company to be a leader. Here is your big chance for the future. What you want to do is head for a cube 1 position. If you make it, you become the new Microsoft. An expensive strategy, but you may look good on the cover of *Business Week*.

Cube 3,

a market situation that many companies prefer over cubes 1 and 2. Some managers are more than willing to accept a lower margin in a relatively unexciting market that will not attract competition like cubes 1 and 2. These are the companies sought out by Peter Lynch, who ran the Fidelity Magellan stock fund for twenty years and compiled the best return for its shareholders among all mutual funds. He stayed away from the hot companies in the glamorous industries and looked for boring markets that had companies with boring names. One of his favorites, and a profitable investment, was a tire company named "Pep Boys—Manny, Moe, and Jack." He said the name was better than dull, it was ridiculous, and the market was equally as dull—or ridiculous. However, the company's earnings kept going up year after year because it was an efficient operation and had little competition.

Cube 4,

similar to cube 2 in that it represents a new market, except that the profit potential is not as great. The advantage is that you are probably not going to get hit over the head by a rush of competitors if your sales start climbing. Just be sure there is enough profit available to make it worth your time.

Cube 5,

a market with strong profit potential and in which you and at least one of your competitors are strong. An example could be the computer workstation market. Until recently, Sun Microsystems enjoyed a number 1 cube market situation (profitable market with no major competitors). Now, however, it must contend with IBM, Hewlett-Packard, Digital Equipment, and a host of clones. Money can still be made in this type of market, but usually conditions are not as favorable as they are in cube 1 or even 3.

Cube 6,

a market where profit potential is high and your competition is strong but you are not. This is like getting into the computer workstation market today from scratch. AT&T tried this approach with personal computers and failed, and General Electric tried it with mainframe computers and also failed. It can be done, but usually you need a new technology to break through. However, in that case you are no longer competing in cube 6. You are starting a new market similar to cube 2 or 4.

These six market situations are where you normally want to position your business. The purpose of strategic planning is to push your company into one of these markets and, if you are already there, to stay competitive in them. If you are a marketing person you want to be where the action is to afford your Corvette (I refuse to make reference here to a Japanese car). Markets 1 and 5 offer the largest marketing budgets because they offer the potential for greater profit margins. If you are in markets in the lower half of the figure (cubes 3, 4, 7, and 8), profit margins are small and there is little room for major marketing efforts. If you begin in cube 2, you won't have much to spend today because you are too small. If you can help push the business into cube 1, you will be repaid for the lean years.

You don't want to participate in cubes 7 and 8, whether you are in marketing or in another area. Cube 7 represents a market offering relatively low margins, with both you and the competition having equal weight. An example is department stores. Cube 8 is similar to cube 7, except that you are weak. This is like entering the steel business.

The eight cube or market positions can be related to

product/service life cycles. The four cubes at the top of the figure depict markets in the introductory or growth stage. Cube 1 is normally a market in early growth; cube 2, introductory; and cubes 5 and 6, late growth. The four cubes at the bottom of the figure can be markets in any of the stages. Cube 4 is introductory; cube 3 can be either growth or maturity; and cubes 7 and 8, either maturity or decline.

Selecting Strategies

After you have completed your situation analysis, your next step is to determine a set of strategies for each business, product, or service for the next three to ten years. This is the third key element in strategic planning.

You may want to position your one or more businesses in its appropriate cube in Figure 1-5 and then consider developing a strategic plan for reducing your investment in businesses in the high-number cubes and increasing your investment in the low-number cubes.

Normally, in cube or market positions 1 through 4, you should go for a bigger piece of the pie or share of market. A market position similar to cube 5 or 7 normally calls for earnings; that is, you just try to maintain your relative market position, assuming that you already have a large share. This strategy should throw off enough cash to help finance the aggressive stance you should be taking for any new businesses in market positions 2 and 4. Market positions 1 and 3 usually can support themselves financially. Market positions 6 and 8 are either new businesses for you or markets in which you are extremely weak and your competition is strong. Both are precarious, and you should give considerable thought to any further investments.

Some of the other strategic strategies you should consider are:

- Vertical integration
- Market segmentation
- Product/service line extension
- Pricing

- Expanding distribution
- Cost efficiency
- Annual product/service modifications
- Promotional expenditures

Vertical integration occurs when you purchase your suppliers (upstream) or your distribution network (downstream). Market segmentation is offering new products or services aimed at particular segments of the market, such as light beer, dry beer, imported beer, and low-alcohol-content beer. Product line extensions are similar to segmentation except that they derive from the existing service. Examples are twenty-four-month CDs and thirty-six-month CDs. Pricing strategy refers to deciding whether to price high to skim off those customers who are less sensitive to price or to price low to appeal to all and try to keep out competition.

Expanding distribution is the process of finding new outlets through which to sell your product or service. Cost efficiency refers to an emphasis on controlling costs. Although cost efficiency is more important today in all market positions because of international competition, it is especially critical in the later stages of the life cycle, when your service is more of a commodity and price is more important to the customer. Examples of annual product modifications are new models for automobiles, refrigerators, and television sets. Service industries do not normally offer annual service modifications, which I believe is a mistake. Promotional expenditures refers to the aggressiveness of the promotional program.

Figure 1-6 provides examples of natural strategies (where the odds are with you) and unnatural strategies (where the odds are against you) in terms of market share and the eight market conditions as your business passes through the various stages of the market life cycle.

It is beyond the scope of this book to go further into the selection of marketing strategies. If you would like to read further on this subject, you may wish to consult my two books on business planning, *How to Develop a Business Plan in 15 Days* (New York: AMACOM, 1987) and *The Start-Up Business Plan* (Englewood Cliffs, N.J.: Prentice-Hall, 1991).

Figure 1-6. Natural strategies for the four stages of the life cycle.

Strategy	Introduction	Growth	Maturity	Decline
Market share	Increase	Increase	Maintain	Maintain
Vertical integration	No	Yes*	Yes*	No
Market segmentation	No	Yes*	Yes*	No
Product line extension	No	Yes*	Yes*	No
Pricing	High	Competitive	Decrease	Low
Distribution	Build	Build	Maintain	Maintain
Cost efficiency	No	No	Yes	Yes
Annual product modifications	No	Yes*	Yes*	Maybe
Promotional expenditures	High	Highest	Low	None

* During late growth–early maturity.

Establishing Controls

After you determine your strategies, the final step is establishment of controls. If one of your strategies is to increase market share, you have to select the mechanism to measure your progress. Controls will be discussed in greater detail in the chapters on research, but three requirements will be mentioned here:

1. Is it needed?
2. Can it be measured?
3. Is it enforceable?

If you have a control that has been in existence more than a couple of years, it probably isn't needed today. Controls should arise out of plans; each time you develop a new plan, you should set a new group of controls. If a control does not apply to the plan, get rid of it.

The controls you choose have to be measurable. To increase sales means nothing; you can't determine whether you met the control. However, an increase in sales of 10 percent is a measurable objective. Set up your controls so that they raise a flag only when you are off target; a control that does something when things go wrong is better than one that measures activity every minute or hour.

In addition, controls must be enforceable. Controls that are not enforceable, like Prohibition, do more harm than good. When you have one or more controls that are unenforceable, employees have a tendency not to pay attention to any of them.

Getting the Plan Approved

After each business unit completes its strategic plan, the plan should be sent to corporate headquarters for approval. No corporation has unlimited financial resources, and it should be the responsibility of top management to decide which strategic business units (SBUs) receive sufficient funding to execute their programs. If a business has one or more brands or SBUs in market positions 5 or 7, it may be able to generate sufficient cash flow on its own to finance aggressive strategies for other products under its control.

Management may also decide to liquidate or sell a business unit because it is relatively unprofitable or to acquire a company or SBU because it has products in the growth stage or in dominant or strong competitive positions.

Management should not set such objectives as a 15 percent ROI and pass them down to the SBUs. A product or service in the introductory stage should never have the same ROI as one in the mature stage. Rather, SBUs should develop their strategic plans as outlined in this chapter, and then top management should decide how corporate finances are to be dispersed.

2

Marketing Personnel

Recurring questions asked by marketing people who attend seminars concern their responsibilities and the relationship between their jobs and other departments in their companies. This chapter provides information to help answer these questions.

The Product or Brand Manager

During the 1930s, 1940s, and even the 1950s, it was not unusual to find one individual in a corporation who had both the responsibility and the authority over sales, advertising, sales promotion, public relations, and new product development. From a marketing person's viewpoint, this is the ideal situation. The title usually was director of marketing, and you will still find this position in many corporations.

However, as corporations grew larger and offered more and more products and services, the management structure of marketing began to change. Two of the major consumer packaged goods companies, Procter & Gamble and General Foods, feared that some of their brands would be lost in the shuffle and not receive the individual attention needed. The brand manager or product manager position was developed to ensure that each brand or product would receive the necessary support from the various functional activities of the business, such as manufacturing, promotion, and sales. However, rather than having the responsibility and the authority for all these activities, as the director of marketing had in the past, the product or brand manager usually had complete control in only one area—promotion. Product and brand managers were responsible for the sales of their brands, but they did not have control of the sales force. Likewise, they were responsible for the profit but did not have complete authority over the manufacturing function.

For this reason, the product or brand management concept failed in many companies. This type of organization is usually best only in multiproduct companies where it is impossible to separate the various functions, such as sales, promotion, and new product development. Before a company sets up a product or brand management structure, it should be sure that this is the best of all possible worlds. If it is, then management has to be sure that there are clearly established lines of communication between the product or brand manager and the various line functions.

The product or brand manager should be in a position to present a written plan to top management once a year. After this document is approved, the manager should have the authority to make most day-to-day operating decisions. The manager should also have an appropriate line of communication directly to the field to be sure that all aspects of the plan are quickly executed. The management tasks of the product manager should include the following:

- Preparing the complete marketing plan
- Establishing measurements and controls
- Communicating the plan to the entire company
- Creating and maintaining enthusiasm for the plan
- Preparing a midyear report to management

The marketing decision areas for which the product manager should have primary responsibility are:

- Product
- Packaging
- Advertising
- Communications research
- Sales promotion

The tasks and decisions of the product manager should .influence the behavior and activities of practically all departments within the company, including engineering, manufacturing, research and development, marketing research, sales and customer service, finance and accounting, data processing, and legal.

The product manager's role with engineering is primarily interpretive. Product managers should convey the needs of the market to engineering as well as monitor the product or service to be sure that changes in function, quality, and design are favorable. To manufacturing, product managers are the source of information about past and anticipated sales volume, which is used for developing production schedules. Product managers should balance market needs against cost in recommending inventory levels and continually feed back information on product performance in the marketplace.

In addition to suggesting market needs and product concepts to research and development, product managers must also evaluate R&D ideas from the viewpoint of market needs. If there isn't close communication between marketing and R&D, the successful new product development rate will be even lower than the pitiful national average of 10 to 30 percent.

The relationship between marketing research and the product manager is covered in Chapter 11, but briefly, the product manager should continually use market research to measure market needs and the satisfaction of those needs by the company's product or service as well as by the competition.

In dealing with sales and customer service, product managers should serve as a source of information on their product line, convince sales to execute the sales portion of the marketing plan, and help train customer service teams as to the functions of the product or service.

Product managers play a major role in obtaining the necessary financial support for the marketing plan from the finance and accounting department. They should develop a thorough knowledge of the profit-and-loss statement, including a concern for net as well as gross profit. They should be on the lookout for arbitrary assignments of administrative or staff charges to the product line. Ideally, product managers should have the right to sign off on all administrative charges. That means that they can reject, for example, an assigned cost of $20,000 from a staff department. Of course, if a product manager rejects the charge, then the service is not provided.

Electronic data processing (EDP) is becoming a more important marketing tool each year. Every product manager should be familiar with what EDP can and cannot do to provide more accurate and timely marketing information. If product managers have no experience with EDP, they should consider attending educational seminars on the subject.

Product managers should always remember that the company's legal department is friend, not foe. All advertising and sales promotion activities should be cleared with this department in their developmental stages to prevent wasted time and expenditures. Remember, you as an individual can be prosecuted for misleading and false advertising claims and be fined or imprisoned, or both. It's not worth the gamble, so always check everything with your legal department.

The Marketing Manager

The marketing manager is very similar to the product or brand manager except that the marketing manager's efforts are devoted to one or more products within one or more market segments. A marketing manager is normally used when a company has many similar or closely related products that are sold to different segments of the market. The marketing manager, like the product or brand manager, is responsible for getting the products to the market, but once again, he or she does not normally have direct line authority over all the various functions required to get the job completed.

The advertising manager is usually responsible only for the advertising function, just as the sales promotion manager is responsible for sales promotion and the public relations director is responsible for public relations.

Many advertising or marketing executives are promoted from field sales and make the mistake of not altering their perspectives to reflect the requirements of their new positions. Salespeople have a tendency to concentrate on sales volume rather than on profit, on the short run rather than on the long run, on individual customers rather than on market segments, and on fieldwork rather than on desk work. Usually they are not attentive to profit differences between products or customer classes. They do not tend to think of product or market expansion strategies over the next three to five years, and they lack in developing strategies for the various marketing segments.

When salespeople are transferred to the marketing operation, they have to alter their planning perspective to include profitability of various products and services, long-run trends, threats and opportunities, customer and segment types, and constant market analysis. They should plan their sales volume around profits; study how to translate market changes into new products, new markets, and new market strategies; determine how to offer superior values to the most profitable product lines; and be familiar with all the financial implications of their marketing plans.

You may be interested in knowing what top management usually considers the basic problems with marketing personnel:

- They fail to provide sufficient factual information and make sound marketing decisions.
- They do not understand the broad implications of marketing, especially relative to return on investment, strategic or long-range planning, financial implications, and manufacturing.
- They spend too much money on advertising, considering that it is not as exact a science as finance and manufacturing.

Conversely, you may enjoy hearing the most commonly voiced complaints of marketing personnel against the people in top management:

- They lack understanding of the marketing function, especially advertising.
- They fail to explain the company's long-range goals and financial objectives.
- They consider themselves advertising experts.

I hope this book will help management and marketing personnel to understand each other's functions.

3

The Advertising Agency

This chapter discusses how to select an advertising agency. If you already have an agency affiliation, this information should allow you to review or critique your current operation. The chapter also provides insight on how an agency should function in its relationship with clients.

If you are looking for a new advertising agency, there is no precise method of compiling a list for subsequent conferences. However, here are a few suggestions. First, analyze the advertising you see. When you notice what you consider an extremely effective campaign, something that really gets you excited, call up the advertiser and ask for the name of its agency. Next, call up the agency president and ask if he or she would be interested in discussing your future advertising plans.

Second, discuss your situation with the various media representatives. Ask them if they are familiar with any agency that appears to be doing excellent work. Media people are very anxious to help clients locate good agencies because it makes their work easier. A happy client makes a happy media rep. Third, go to your local advertising club. In some cities, the ad club offers a good representation of the better agencies. In others, it is primarily a concentration of advertising suppliers looking for sales prospects. The problem is you never know until you go to a couple of meetings.

If none of the above work, you may have to send out letters of inquiry to all the advertising agencies in your vicinity. Send each a letter telling about your corporation, possibly including one or two of your major marketing problems. Then ask if the agency would be interested in discussing a possible relationship. From subsequent telephone and written communications, pare the initial list down to three to five agencies for further discussion. At this point, you should either invite the agencies to your company or set up appointments in their offices. In these discussions, five factors should be examined: management, account service, media department, creative team, and compensation. These are discussed in the following paragraphs.

Management

Managing an advertising agency is difficult. There are two distinctly different types of people employed by an agency, and they are not always compatible. There are the account, media, and research people, and there are the creative people. The former are not unlike people you find in most companies; the latter are unique. They tend to resist organization, conventional dress, and higher authority. Don't be disturbed by the different life-styles. It is not unusual that the most unconventional creative people perform the best. The key you should look for is agency management that can put these two seemingly incompatible groups together in a structure where one does not dominate the other and neither loses its identity or contribution. It's not easy.

If the creative group dominates, and it does in many agencies, then you usually find weak account, media, and research teams. In this situation, it is not uncommon for a creative person to show an ad to the account executive and the account executive to state that it's the wrong approach. The creative person ignores this and instructs the account executive to show the client the ad and return immediately so production can begin. The account executive, possibly afraid of losing his or her job, shows the client the ad, stating that it's perfect for the current marketing situation. Many clients, not having the benefit of previous advertising experience and assuming that what is presented has the approval of all the professionals at the agency, approve the ad.

The converse is also true: An agency can be dominated by

the account people. Many good creative people will not work in such an environment. Excellent advertising campaigns can be vetoed by the account executive because of politics or lack of imagination before the client ever gets the opportunity to see the ads.

Ask the management of each advertising agency you are interviewing how it would handle disagreement between the creative and the account groups over whether the creative work should be presented to the client. Any agency that appears to be dominated by one side or the other should be eliminated at this time.

Account Service

The marketing expertise of an advertising agency can be invaluable to a client. The marketing people are called account executives, account supervisors, and management supervisors. The account executives report to the account supervisors, who in turn report to the management supervisors.

Preferably, the account people should have MBAs. There is no comparison between courses offered in undergraduate schools and those in master's programs, either in content or in the qualifications of the professors. A considerable amount of the material presented in a good graduate school can be used immediately in the day-to-day operations of a business. Many of the larger advertising agencies will no longer hire an account executive without an MBA.

You should also look for account people who have had experience solving marketing problems similar to yours. This does not necessarily mean that they should have past experience in your industry. Sometimes it is better that they don't. Too much familiarity can lead to stagnation. What it does mean is that if you are number one in the industry, look for an account group that has handled another client that was the leader. If you are a discounter, look for experience with other discount stores. If you are a quality operation, look for experience with other quality lines or stores.

As stated in Chapter 1, products and services in the same competitive position, regardless of the industry, have similar natural marketing strategies. That's the benefit of working with agency people—they're people from the outside with marketing experience in executing strategies that are also natural to your business. A good account team can also provide a much broader range of marketing activities than you would ever be able to obtain internally. No matter how hard you try, after years with a particular corporation, you develop tunnel vision. It's up to your account team to constantly broaden the perspective.

Liaison between your corporation and the advertising agency is another responsibility of the account people. You should be able to discuss with them all your marketing problems, and it is up to them to get you the right help from the agency. If you are having problems with other people within the agency, it is the account group that you go to for clarification and corrective action.

For these reasons, there has to be the right chemistry between you and the account group. Don't select an agency that offers an account group you don't feel comfortable with. You can usually tell when you first meet people if there is going to be a personality conflict. If you think there is, stay away from those people.

Your account group is also responsible for providing agency assistance in the development of your marketing plan. The account group should help determine your marketing strategies and plans and provide you with the services of all other agency departments. For example, the media department should help prepare your media strategy, the creative group the creative strategy, and the production people your production budget.

Media

The media department of an advertising agency is responsible for the development and execution of your media strategy and plan. (These are discussed in Chapter 7.) The media function has become much more complex in recent years. One of the reasons is the segmentation of the various media. Radio stations are constantly developing new formats to gain a niche in the listening audience. There are all-talk, all-jazz, and many other unique styles. A station may be folk music today and Spanish-American music tomorrow. There is also the division between AM and FM. In the Los Angeles region alone, there are twenty-eight AM and thirty-eight FM stations.

Magazine and newspaper publishers have also been forced to appeal to specific groups within the reading audience in order to stay alive in the television era. Gone are general-interest magazines, because they were competing directly with television and couldn't win the numbers game. In their place have come the magazines directed at particular life-styles. Today, there are magazines for every interest group, from organic gardeners to owners of small businesses. Not only do the big daily newspapers publish regional editions to compete with the growth of the suburban papers, but they've developed special sections on science, cooking, travel, gardening, and health. These are in addition to the other sections, such as business and sports, that they have had for years.

Buying time or space for radio, magazine, and newspaper advertising is complicated today, but it may be a piece of cake compared to what buying for television will be like in the future. Already you have the superstations, such as Ted Turner's Atlanta operation—the signal is bounced off satellites for coast-to-coast programming. Though the price is still quite high, homeowners can now buy their own miniature earth stations. These highly powerful antennas pick up practically any television station in the country. For the near term, though, cable television has the fastest growth. In 1991, about 60 percent of all U.S. homes were hooked up. What does all this mean? It will become increasingly difficult to decide where you will get the best return for your advertising dollar.

When reviewing various advertising agencies, you should ask to meet the media people who will be working on your account. Sadly, some still buy time and space depending on who bought them lunch, dinner, or drinks the previous day. But most media people do not operate this way, and it's best to avoid those who do.

You should ask the media people about the innovative media plans they have developed for other clients. Also ask about their accessibility to computer data banks and their ability to program for the optimum media schedule for your account.

Don't overlook the importance of the media department. You can have a great creative campaign, but if it is being seen by the wrong people or with insufficient frequency, what good is it? Also, a sharp media buyer with experience is able to buy media time and space at rates lower than those shown on the rate cards. With the cost of media increasing 10 to 20 percent each year, you need all the experience and ingenuity you can get just to stay even.

Creative Group

The creative group, more than any other group in the agency, can make or break you. These people have the most influence over whether you get a dull campaign or one that is clever and catchy. Never select an agency until you meet the creative team that will work on your account. Don't buy the common line, "We have many fantastic copywriters and art directors, and you'll get the best." Ask who they will be, and look at their work. If you're not enthusiastic about what you see, then don't use that agency.

You should also make it clear that you want to see creative work done by employees still with the agency. Agency employees, especially the creative staff, change jobs frequently. If you're not careful, you might select an agency on the basis of creative work done by people no longer with the firm.

Compensation

There are basically three factors that influence the amount of money an advertising agency should be paid. First is the number of ads that have to be prepared relative to the total budget. Obviously, it costs an agency more in time and overhead expenses to prepare ten ads for a $500,000 budget than to prepare five ads. This is one of the reasons that industrial advertisers generally have to pay their agencies a greater percentage of the total budget than consumer advertisers. Media costs for industrial trade publications are much lower than for consumer magazines. This means more insertions per media dollar, which in turn means a greater number of ads. Industrial advertisers also usually have a greater diversity of products or services. Once again, this means a larger number of ads.

The second determining factor is the number of agency services the client uses. A request for "full service" means the client is using the services of the account team, the creative group, the media department, the production department, and the traffic department. These five services are normally provided if a client is paying on the standard commission basis, as discussed later.

When you do not use the agency's media department, you can lower your payments to the agency by 25 to 33 percent. Some clients use just the creative services; others use just the account group and the creative services. In these situations, clients pay the agencies less money, but, of course, they have to find somebody else to do the work the agency did not do.

The third factor that influences agency compensation is the number of approval levels that are required within the client's organization. In some corporations, only one person has to approve the agency's copy, layout, mechanicals, negatives, and proofs. In others, there can be as many as three or four approval levels. For example, the agency may have to present first to the advertising manager, then come back and present to the director of marketing. A third or fourth meeting may be necessary for discussion with top management. Under these conditions, considerably more agency time is required. Remember, all an agency has to sell is its time and expertise. Its complete inventory walks out the door each night and returns the next morning.

There are three primary methods of compensating an agency: commission, retainer or fee, and cost-plus. With the commission system, the agency receives a certain percentage of the media budget. The amount was originally set at 15 percent, but today, on a national average, consumer advertisers pay 14 percent and industrial advertisers 21 percent. Most media give agencies a 15 percent discount off their rate cards for time or space. They are called commissionable media. What this means is that if the cost of an ad is $1,000, the agency is charged only $850. If a client has hired an agency on the 15 percent commission basis, the agency would bill the client $1,000 and send a check to the advertising medium for $850. If the client is on a 20 percent commission basis, the agency would bill the client $1,062 and pay the medium $850. The reason the amount is $1,062 rather than $1,050 is that agencies always take their commissions on the gross amount, not the net.

This does not mean that advertising agencies are the only ones that can receive discounts from advertising media. In years past it did, but this is no longer true. Today, it is illegal for any advertising medium to pay agency commissions to advertising agencies and refuse to give the same discount to the advertiser.

When an agency is on a retainer or fee basis, it receives a set amount of money each month. It then returns to the client all commissions paid by the media. That is, if a medium gives the agency a 15 percent discount on a $1,000 ad, the agency bills the client only $850. Some clients are on a combination of commission and retainer or fee. This happens when the agency cannot make a sufficient profit on just the commissions, which sometimes occurs with industrial accounts or clients with small media budgets.

Most clients are surprised that many agencies prefer the retainer or fee compensation system rather than the commission basis. The reason is that it gives them a known amount of revenue each month. It can be difficult to operate an advertising agency with all accounts on the commission system because of the erratic cash flow. Agencies on the commission system can bill their clients only when the advertising runs. This can result in such wide swings as $500,000 in revenues one month and only $100,000 the next.

There are agencies, though, that still prefer the commission basis. The rationale is that they should be rewarded when they do good work; if they do good work, the client will increase the budget, and they will then receive more money. One advertiser increased the media budget from $300,000 to $3 million within two years because the results were so spectacular. If the agency had been on the commission basis, its revenues would have increased 1,000 percent. If it had been on a retainer, at least theoretically, its revenue increase would have been zero.

The third and newest way to pay an advertising agency is on a cost-plus basis. The agency adds up all its expenses, including rent, taxes, salaries, utilities, and other operating costs. Then you are billed for your share of the agency's total expenditures plus a predetermined profit.

What you should consider when determining how to compensate your agency is asking them which method they prefer. If they opt for the commission basis and you have no problem, then let it be commissions. If you think they will inflate budget requests if on commissions, then ask for their second choice. The important point is to select a means of payment that is acceptable to both client and agency.

Regardless of whether the client is on a commission system, retainer or fee basis, or cost-plus, the agency will also bill the advertiser for production costs plus agency commission on out-of-pocket expenditures. Except for advertisers with very small budgets, the services of the account group are included in the commission system or retainer and not in the production costs. This is usually true for the copywriter, also. However, most agencies include the art director's time in the production invoice. If an art director spends three hours preparing layouts for an ad and is billed out at $50 an hour, then the client will receive a bill for $150. Also billed as a production cost is mechanical time—that is, the hours spent by agency personnel to paste type, artwork, and so on down on boards (called mechanicals) for preparation of negatives and proofs.

In addition to the costs of the art director and mechanical time, the agency will bill the client for all out-of-pocket expenses—for typography, artwork, photography, engravings, negatives, and proofs. The agency will also charge a commission on the out-of-pocket expenses, usually 17.65 percent. The reason for such an odd figure is that if agencies charged 15 percent on out-of-pocket expenditures, they would not be receiving the same rate of return as they do on media expenses. On an ad with a media cost of $1,000, the agency makes 15 percent, or $150. However, on the agency's actual out-of-pocket expense of $850, $150 is 17.65 percent.

On production bills, you should demand details on all

expenditures, including duplicate invoices from all suppliers. If there is a $300 photography charge, then attached to the bill should be a duplicate copy of the invoice from the photographer in the amount of $300. Clients that allow agencies to send them summary billing, such as $1,000 for copy, layout, mechanical time, and artwork, are offering the agency the opportunity to take a greater markup. It may be the rare agency that takes advantage of such an opportunity, but requiring itemized bills protects you against such agencies.

Making the Selection

After you have reviewed the five factors (management, account group, media department, creative team, and system of compensation) with your final selection of three to five agencies, you should be in a good position to select the one that is best for you.

Be careful about requesting speculative presentations. First, it's expensive for the agencies, and the best ones usually will not participate. Second, the agencies don't know enough about your business at this point to advise you. If you buy their recommendations and they don't know if what they are saying is really right, then the one who suffers is you. Third, when agencies are asked to make speculative presentations, they sometimes hire creative talent from the outside. What they present may be spectacular, but after the agency gets the account, you may never see this creative talent again.

Base your selection on the agency people you meet—the people who will be working on your account. You can tell if they know what they are doing. Pick the best group—that should be your agency.

The Client-Agency Relationship

Now that you have selected an agency, you should make everything it needs available to it. You have probably heard it before, but it's true—a client-agency relationship is like a marriage. If you start withholding information from each other,

Figure 3-1. Agency evaluation form.

	Evaluation _____ Position _____ Date _____				
	5	4	3	2	1
I. Overall Performance					
A. Marketing					
General Knowledge					
Product knowledge					
Strageties					
Plans					
B. Creative					
Development					
Execution					
Scheduling					
C. Media Plan					
General knowledge					
Specific product area					
Development of plan					
Execution of plan					
Budget control					
D. Others					

(continues)

Figure 3-1. Continued.

II. Personnel Performance (rating 5 - 1)

	Account Group	Copy Group	Media Group	Market Research	Other
Imaginative	——	——	——	——	——
Takes initiative	——	——	——	——	——
Able to communicate	——	——	——	——	——
Cost efficient	——	——	——	——	——
Reliable	——	——	——	——	——
Cooperative	——	——	——	——	——
Professional	——	——	——	——	——

III. Strengths and Weaknesses

IV. Recommendations for Improvement

if you are not credible to each other, a divorce will be forthcoming.

An example of how *not* to treat your agency comes from a person who was actually trying to show the disadvantage of in-house agencies. He said that whenever he had a critical deadline, it was difficult to make his own in-house creative director work over the weekend. Here was a person he had lunch with two or three times a week; on the weekends, their families even socialized together. How could he ask him to spend Saturday and Sunday in the office? Now, he concluded, if he had an agency, he would just pick up the phone, call the agency, and tell the people there that if he didn't have the ad by Monday morning, he would find another agency.

No wonder he had an in-house agency. Probably no respectable agency would work for him. Antics like this destroy productive work between client and agency. Reward your agency when it does good work, and criticize it when it is sloppy and ineffectual. Many clients have a formal rating procedure that they use with their agencies. Some companies that have several agencies subject them to extensive performance reviews each year. If any of the agencies comes in last two years in a row, the company has the prerogative of firing it. Actually, most agencies prefer this type of review to sporadic, nonproductive criticism. Figure 3-1 shows an agency rating format that you can adapt to your own particular needs.

4

The Fact Book

The soundness of a strategic plan depends on the completeness of the situation analysis (discussed in Chapter 1), and the soundness of a marketing plan depends on the completeness of the fact book. The situation analysis provides all the facts you need to know about the market, the competition, the customer, and your own resources to determine in which direction you plan to take each business unit and which resources are needed to get you there. The strategic plan is long-term and covers all facets of the business.

After you develop the strategic plan, you should complete a set of shorter-term and more specific plans for each function of the business, such as R&D, engineering, manufacturing, operations, financial, administration, and marketing. Each of these functional plans should be supported by pertinent data. The data required for the development of a marketing plan are referred to in this book as the fact book. The fact book should cover the same four subjects as the situation analysis but should focus primarily on their relationship to marketing. Figures 4-1 through 4-4 provide some indication of the scope of the fact book.

The Market

Figure 4-1 discusses aspects of the market. The first factor, size of the market, indicates the amount of marketing coverage needed; the second, growth, shows how much you have to expand each year to maintain your current share. The third factor, number of competitors, reveals how many competitors

Figure 4-1. Fact book: market.

A. Market

    1. Size
    2. Growth
    3. Number of Competitors
    4. Market Shares
    5. R&D
    6. Pricing Sensitivity
    7. Captive Customers
    8. Barriers to Entry
    9. Economies of Scale
   10. Regulatory Exposure
   11. Opportunity to Segment
   12. Potential for Functional Substitution
   13. Aggressiveness of Competitors

Apply a value to each factor, positive or negative, to determine the profit potential of the market relative to other markets in which you compete.

---

you have to second-guess about marketing strategies. The fourth factor, market shares of competitors, indicates the strength of each of the players. The fifth factor, R&D, tells you the amount of new products/services that will probably be coming on the market. The sixth factor, pricing sensitivity, reveals how important price will be to the customer; the seventh factor, captive customers, tells you both whether the competition has some customers locked up so well that you can't take them away and whether you have the ability to lock some up yourself.

The eighth factor, barriers to entry, indicates whether you will face a bunch of new competitors if you start to make good money (i.e, whether your field, like real estate, has low entrance barriers) or whether it will be difficult for new players to enter because of high capital costs, such as in auto manufacturing (i.e., whether there are high entrance barriers). The ninth factor, economies of scale, indicates whether a large competitor with many stores or extensive coverage can benefit from reduced production or marketing costs and apply the same marketing pressure as you can, but at greatly reduced expenditures. The tenth factor, regulatory exposure, reveals the extent of legal clearance required for marketing activities. The eleventh factor, opportunity to segment, tells you the number of market segments you will have to address in your marketing program. The twelfth factor, potential of functional distribution, indicates how critical it will be for your product or service to be perceived as superior to potential substitutes; if you are marketing snowblowers, you have to convince customers that shoveling by hand is simply out of the question. The thirteenth factor, aggressiveness of competitors, tells you just how tough it will be to make a buck and how strong your marketing program has to be.

You should analyze the marketing opportunity in each of your markets, using some or all of these factors plus any additional ones you believe are pertinent. You can use a scoring system of positives and negatives, a scale ranging from one to ten, or some other type of analysis that permits you to rank your various markets in the order of opportunity to maximize market share or earnings. Then go on to Figure 4-2, which helps you to examine the strengths of your competitors.

Competitors

The first factor listed in Figure 4-2 is business philosophy. This factor refers to how competitors will act or counteract in a market. What is their pricing philosophy? Will they continuously cut prices? If you increase or decrease your price, will they follow? Are they more likely to go for market share or earnings? If you double your marketing budget, will they match the increase? Whenever you are developing a strategy, you always want to ask yourself whether you think your competition will follow. If the answer is yes, you probably don't want to use that strategy. If you double your marketing budget and the competition matches it, where are you? Worse off. If you cut your price and they match it, where are you? Worse off. That is why knowing your competition's business philosophy is so important: You always want to develop strate-

Figure 4-2. Fact book: competitors.

B. Competitors

1. Business Philosophy
2. R&D Expenditures
3. Number of New Products/Services
4. Marketing Communications
5. Sales Force
6. Customer Service
7. Depth of Line
8. Distribution
9. Quality
10. Capital

Write a scenario for each major competitor, taking into account the above marketing factors.

This critique should help in determining where competition is least likely to follow.

gies that the competition is least likely to follow. Knowing ahead of time how you believe it will react is very helpful in achieving this objective.

The rest of the factors in Figure 4-2 refer to the various components of competitors' businesses. What you are trying to ascertain is where they are strong and where they are weak. This information will help you determine whether they have the critical factors necessary in a particular market to become or stay strong, and can also help you figure out how to attack their weaknesses. If the critical strengths in one of your markets are advertising, sales promotion, distribution, and depth of line (number of sizes, shapes, models, etc.), you don't want to spend considerable marketing dollars slugging it out against a competitor who is an expert in these fields. You may be able to develop a marvelously new soap or toothpaste, but do you really want to fight Procter & Gamble? I doubt it. Or, you may have a great idea for a new amusement park. Market characteristics (Figure 4-1) could look favorable, but, when you analyze competitive strengths, you should realize that you have to locate far away from a Disney property. The critical strength in this market is customer service, and Disney is unmatchable in its execution.

The Customer

Figure 4-3 contains some factors you can use to study customer needs in each of your markets and to determine whether you can meet them. You should start by defining who is the customer. By using demographics, psychographics, Standard Industrial Classifications (SIC), or some other form of identification, you should identify the approximately 20 percent of all potential customers who will account for at least 80 percent of your profit. This can be called your target audience. Demographics are statistical classifications, such as age, income, sex, education, and geographical location. Psychographics identify people by life-style or personality. You don't want to use the same marketing tools or messages to reach the Henry Kissingers of the world (former secretary of state under President Nixon) as you would to reach the Willard Scotts (weatherman on the morning NBC news program *Today*). SIC codes are set up by the federal government and are used to define various industries, as well as job descriptions within these industries.

Using one of these identification methods, you want to

Figure 4-3. Fact book: customers.

C. Customer

1. Target Audience
2. Benefits Sought
3. Conversion Awareness to Trial
4. Percent 1st Repeat, 2nd Repeat, etc.
5. Amount Trial, Amount Repeat in Currency/Units
6. Customer Loyalty

Determine a profile on the 20% of your customers who should account for 80% of your profit.

---

locate the approximately 20 percent of total
who purchase so much more than the ave
count for at least 80 percent of the total volu
quantity price discounts, provide 80 perce
Young, blue-collar workers account for appro
cent of all beer drinkers but drain over 80 perce   ⌐ ˎˏ˖ˍ˖ˍ˖ˍ,
glasses, and cans. In almost every market, regardless of the
type of product or service, from soap to computers, from hotels
to insurance, this concentration of frequent buyers prevails.
You have to know who these customers are and provide what
they want if you expect to be a major factor in a market.

The second factor in Figure 4-3 addresses what customers
want. What are the benefits they are seeking, and what features does your product/service have to deliver these benefits?
If young people who own sporty cars want a radar detector to
avoid the police, your unit has to be able to peek around
corners, trees, and hills. No radar detector does this better than
Cincinnati Microwave's Passport; no wonder it's the market
leader. Chemical Bank in New York decided it could not compete against huge competitors like Citibank in offering financial
services to major corporations, so it went after the medium-
size-company niche, seeking out companies that believed the
major banks treated them like second-class citizens. Chemical
developed a marketing program aimed directly at the needs of
medium-size companies and now is the market leader in this
segment.

Factor three is estimated conversion awareness to trial.
This refers to the percentage of potential customers who become aware of your service that will purchase your item the
first time. Obviously, the higher this percentage, the more
profitable the business. This is the reason you should use a
benchmark study (discussed in Chapter 11) to measure the
level of conversion each year, as well the other factors discussed in this chapter. If you are obtaining low awareness
levels, then your marketing communications plan should be
changed. If you are obtaining high awareness levels but a low
conversion rate, then you should examine the rest of the
marketing mix, including factors such as pricing, distribution,
sales force, packaging, and product quality.

Factor four is repeat business: Of those who try to purchase your service one time, what percentage repeats a second, third, or more times? The percentage of potential customers that tries your product is important, but the percentage that repeats is even more critical. Your sales can be going up due to first-time purchases, leading you to load up on inventory, maybe add to your staff—and then all of a sudden, you may find that sales drop precipitously because no one is repurchasing. Normally, when you have low repeat business, it is not your marketing communications that are at fault but rather the quality of the product or customer service; for example, many people stopped buying American automobiles because U.S. cars kept falling apart. On the other hand, the quality may be good, but the customer service bad.

The fifth factor in Figure 4-3 is the amount customers purchase each time they buy. Here is an opportunity to dramatically increase sales with little or no additional cost. It should not cost any more to sell two units to a customer rather than just one. You should determine the average number of units purchased and then, in your marketing plan, develop strategies for increasing the amount. Sometimes all you need to do is train your people to suggest multiple purchases. Sales promotion is another excellent tool; an example is "Buy two, get the third at half price."

The sixth factor is customer loyalty. Through the use of a benchmark study, you should try to determine what percentage of your current and potential customers switch brands when a special price or deal is offered and then return to the brand they normally purchase after the deal is pulled; what percentage buy only deal merchandise; and what percentage stay loyal to a brand regardless of special offers by the competition.

This information can be very helpful in developing your marketing plan. If you are in a market with low brand loyalty, you might consider developing new strategies to strengthen your brand loyalty. Cigarettes, soft drinks, and beer are all basically commodities; within their industries they all taste pretty much the same. However, Marlboro, Budweiser, and Coca-Cola have each developed a fierce brand loyalty through effective advertising. This has not been true for many areas, including banking, airline travel, and paper products. In these markets, whoever has the hot price gets the business. Whether this dependence on price is due to ineffective marketing or the inherent nature of the market is open to question. If you have tried to build service loyalty in the past without success, then sales promotion will become a more important tool than advertising.

The Product/Service and the Company

Figure 4-4 illustrates the type of information about your own product/service, communications, and company that you

Figure 4-4. Fact book: product/service and company.

D. Product/Service and Company

Write a scenario on your own p/s and company, considering where you are strong and where you are weak on the following marketing factors:

Product/Service

1. Quality
2. Distribution
3. Pricing
4. Depth of Line
5. Features
6. Benefits
7. Positioning

Communications

1. Awareness and Preference
2. Recall and Registration of Sales Message
3. Intent to Buy

Company

1. R&D, Engineering, Manufacturing, Operations
2. Costs
3. Sales Force and Customer Service
4. Business Philosophy

---

should put in your fact book. There are seven factors listed under the product/service subhead. You should cover how your product quality compares with that of the competition, your coverage of the market or level of distribution, and pricing strategy (whether you skim—charge a premium price to skim off people who are less susceptible to price—or penetrate—charge a competitive price and go after the entire market). You should also include a statement on how you will react if the competition raises or lowers its price. It is better to make this decision now, when you have time to think it through, than to act in haste when and if you are confronted with this ploy.

Also listed under product/service, depth of line refers to such things as the number of sizes, shapes, models, and colors you offer. Features describe the service; benefits are what the product does for the customer. To be successful, you have to deliver the benefits the customer is seeking. Positioning is how you want to be perceived by the customer compared to your competition. An example of effective positioning is Marriott Hotels. Bill Marriott positioned his chain right between Hyatt and Holiday Inn. He offered fewer amenities than Hyatt but more than Holiday Inn, with a room charge also in the middle. This positioning appealed to both business travelers and company controllers. Business travelers preferred a Hyatt, but the company objected to the cost; comptrollers suggested the Holiday Inn. They compromised on the Marriott.

There are three factors listed under the communications subhead. Awareness and preference refers to the percentage of people in the market that are aware of what you have to offer, and what percentage prefer you to your competition. Recall and registration of your sales message is the percentage that can play back your message when asked. Recall refers to the percentage that can remember the message in general terms, and registration is the percentage that remember the specific sales points or benefits you were presenting. Intend to buy is the percentage that actually plan on purchasing your product in the near future.

If you obtain low scores on awareness, your marketing communications are probably boring. If you have high awareness but low preference, you are getting the attention of potential buyers, but what you can do for them is probably not coming across, perhaps because your sales message is not registering. If you are obtaining high scores on recall and registration and still getting low preference, either your message is wrong or your communications are on target but some other part of your marketing mix is at fault, perhaps price, packaging, or depth of line. There are so many individual components in your marketing mix that if you don't measure as many as possible, you will never know which ones are working and which ones are not.

The third subhead, company, covers all other activities that affect marketing and that are not included in other parts of the fact book. The first factor is devoted to an analysis of the company compared to the competition, focusing on all other departments or functions of the business. This discussion leads to factor two—costs. You need to determine your position and your competition's on the production curve (discussed in Chapter 1). If you are farther down the curve, you should probably price your product or service lower than your competition's or spend more on R&D or marketing, going for increased market share. If you are further back on the curve, your marketing program has to convince the customer that you have a superior service worth the premium price.

The third factor covers two other components of marketing—sales force and customer service. Do you have an aggressive and professional sales team, as IBM did in the past, or one that appears to lack direction, like Digital Equipment Corporation? Does your customer service department act like that of the typical hotel, airline, retail store, or public utility, whose staff believes it is the customer and that you, the customer, are a pain in the neck? Or have you been successful in exploiting this invaluable marketing tool like Stew Leonard? Mr. Leonard runs his grocery store under the motto "One: The customer is always right; two: If you believe the customer is wrong, refer to number one." It is no surprise that his grocery store is the most profitable in the country.

The fourth factor is business philosophy. This analysis should be similar to factor one in the section on competition, except that now you are critiquing your own company.

The sections and factors discussed in this chapter on the fact book are not meant to be all-inclusive, and you may want to rearrange the order in which they have been presented. What is important is that you include all the factors that impact on the development of your marketing plan. When the author used to compile fact books for clients, the books numbered between 200 and 300 pages. In developing a marketing plan, it is not writing the plan that takes the most time; it is the compilation of the fact book. If you put together a sound fact book, your chances of developing a sound marketing plan are greatly increased. If your fact book is weak, your plan will be weak, also.

After you and your staff have completed the fact book, you are ready for your first meeting to develop the plan. This is the subject of Chapter 5.

Section II

Product/Service Plan

5

Using "What If" Models to Set Marketing Objectives

This is the first of five sections that focus on the five components of marketing: product/service plan, marketing communications plan, research plan, customer relations plan, and sales plan. After the fact book is completed (see Chapter 4), a representative from each of the five component departments should be selected as a member of the planning team for the purpose of developing a marketing plan for a particular market.

The analysis of the market and the competition and the strengths of the business as detailed in the fact book determine the aggressiveness of the marketing plan. The analysis of the customer determines which marketing tools should be used to induce trial and repeat purchases of the company's brand. Can the customer be reached most efficiently through use of the sales team or brochures? How about trade shows or advertising? Should a combination of four or five tools be tried? How should the service be packaged and distributed and in what colors, sizes, and shapes? How will you use customer service and other marketing weapons to ensure a high rate of repeat purchases? How will you use research to continually monitor the aspects of the market as well as the effectiveness of your marketing campaign?

The purpose of this section and the four following sections (comprising Chapters 5 to 15) is to help you develop methods for answering these types of questions. Chapter 16 is devoted to pulling all these activities together in your marketing plan.

The first section or marketing component to be discussed is the product/service plan. The product/service plan should cover such subjects as pricing strategy, packaging, and the number of sizes, shapes, and models that will be offered. Either this plan or the marketing communications plan should cover estimated awareness and preference levels; either this plan, the marketing communications plan, or the sales plan should project conversion awareness to trial and repeat purchase rate. Either this plan or the sales plan should detail unit and dollar sales and market share.

A marvelous tool for tying all these factors together is the "what if" model. A what-if model allows you to select one or more major objectives, such as volume and resulting market share. These objectives go at the end of the model and all the assumptions, variables, or factors that you believe will influence these objectives are inserted in front of them. You then develop mathematical equations that indicate how the various assumptions interact with the objectives. If you structure the model correctly, obtaining the assumption levels you use in your model should deliver the resulting major objectives.

Installing a what-if model on a computer enables you to make changes in variables, automatically revising the objectives by the use of computer formulas. However, if you are not into computers, you can use a calculator or even do your revisions with a pencil and sheet of paper.

You don't need models or other types of mathematical equations to develop an effective marketing plan. However, some people like models and equations, and if you are one of them, you may want to spend the time weeding through the rest of this chapter. It may be difficult because you'll have to keep referring back and forth between the text and the figures (models).

If you wish, you may want just to read the text to examine the thought process on how various marketing factors interrelate and can influence the final outcome of your plan. The main point is that you need some method to determine how a change in one marketing factor will influence others. Often it can be dramatic. To illustrate: Two plans are used in the model;

plan 2 is just slightly more optimistic than plan 1, but results in a market share projection that is approximately 50 percent higher. (To see this, compare Figures 5-6 and 5-7 of the model.)

The model consists of seven sections (Figures 5-1 to 5-7), with the major objectives being sales volume and market share. These seven sections are as follows:

Figure	*Section*	*Title*
5-1	One	Trial transactions, plans 1 and 2
5-2	Two	Repeat purchasing, plan 1
5-3	Three	Repeat purchasing, plan 2
5-4	Four	Unit and dollar volume, plan 1
5-5	Five	Unit and dollar volume, plan 2
5-6	Six	Share of market, plan 1
5-7	Seven	Share of market, plan 2

Trial Transactions

The first part of the model is shown in Figure 5-1. There are six assumptions. The first is "A. Total number of potential buyers." This is the total number of potential buyers in your market for the type of service you and your competitors sell. Ten thousand is shown.

The second is "B. Conversion awareness to trial, plan 1." This is the percentage of the potential buyers who become aware of your product who you believe will subsequently try to purchase it. The figure 25 percent is shown. Assumption three, "C. Conversion awareness to trial, plan 2," is the same as assumption two, except the data are for plan 2. Thirty percent is used.

Assumption four, "D. Potential buyers aware, plan 1," is the percent of potential buyers that you expect to become aware of your brand over a period of time. Column D shows the awareness climbing to 40 percent by the end of the first year. Assumption five (column E) shows the same type of data for plan 2. For this more optimistic plan, awareness reaches 50 percent. Assumption six is "F. Distribution." Distribution is the percent of your market in which the potential customer can

Figure 5-1. Setting market objectives: trial transactions plans 1 and 2.

	Assumptions		Assumptions
A. Total Number Potential Buyers	10,000	D. Potential Buyers Aware, Plan 1	Shown below
B. Conversion Awareness to Trial Plan 1	25%	E. Potential Buyers Aware, Plan 2	Shown below
C. Conversion Awareness to Trial Plan 2	30%	F. Distribution Level	Shown below

	Awareness				Trial		
Month	D. Potential Buyers Aware, Plan 1 (%)	E. Potential Buyers Aware, Plan 2 (%)	G. Newly Aware, Plan 1	H. Newly Aware, Plan 2	F. Distribution	I. New Trial, Plan 1	J. New Trial, Plan 2
0	0	0	0	0	10	0	0
1	5	5	500	500	30	38	45
2	8	10	300	500	40	30	60
3	13	20	500	1,000	50	63	150
4	16	25	300	500	60	45	90
5	19	30	300	500	70	53	105
6	22	34	300	400	80	60	96
7	25	38	300	400	90	68	108
8	28	42	300	400	90	68	108
9	31	44	300	200	90	68	54
10	34	46	300	200	90	68	54
11	37	48	300	200	90	68	54
12	40	50	300	200	90	68	54
Total			4,000	5,000		693	978

easily and conveniently buy what you sell. If your store or sales force cover 50 percent of the territory, you have a 50 percent distribution level. The same distribution goal is used for both plans for simplicity. The distribution level for this model, shown in column F, increases to 90 percent by the end of the first year. When you put together your own model, if you use two plans, you may want to show different goals for each.

To calculate the number of potential customers who become aware of the product for plan 1, you multiply assumption A (total number of potential customers) by assumption D, as shown in column D (potential buyers aware, plan 1 [%]); for plan 2, multiply assumption A by assumption E as shown in column E (potential buyers aware, plan 2 [%]). The answers are in column G (newly aware, plan 1) and column H (newly aware, plan 2). At the end of twelve months, 4,000 potential buyers become aware of the service for plan 1, and 5,000 for plan 2.

To calculate the number of buyers who will try the brand for plan 1, you multiply column G (newly aware, plan 1) by assumption B (conversion awareness to trial, plan 1) and the resulting answer by assumption F (distribution level) as shown in column F. For example, during the first month, 500 buyers become aware of the product (column G), of whom it is estimated that 25 percent (assumption B) will try the brand. If the company had 100 percent distribution, that would mean that 125 customers would purchase (500 times 25 percent). However, the company has only 30 percent distribution at this time, so you have to multiply 125 by 30 percent, which gives you thirty-eight buyers for month one as shown in column 1 (new trial, plan 1). For plan 2, you multiply column H (newly aware, plan 2) by assumption C (conversion awareness to trial, plan 2), and then multiply the result by assumption F (distribution level), as shown in column F. The answer is in column J (new trial, plan 2). For plan 1, it is calculated that 693 customers will purchase by the end of the year (column I), and for plan 2 (column J), 978 customers. Notice the substantial increase in trial by just increasing the awareness level of 40 percent and the conversion to trial rate of 25 percent in plan 1 to 50 percent awareness and conversion to 30 percent in plan 2. These changes produce a 41 percent gain (from 693 to 978). Relatively small improvements in your marketing plan can have a dramatic effect on your bottom line.

Repeat Purchasing

Sections two and three cover repeat purchasing for plans 1 and 2 and are shown in Figures 5-2 and 5-3. If you have a service that the buyer purchases only once, you would skip this part of the model. For plan 1, the first assumption is "K. Average repeat purchase rate." This is the amount of time a buyer stays out of the market in between purchases and could be a week for coffee, six months for a suit, or two years for a computer. Two months is the figure used in the model. The second assumption is "L. Percentage triers repeat once (%)." This is the percentage of those buyers that tried the brand that you expect will make a second purchase. A figure of 50 percent is used in the model. The two remaining assumptions in this section are the same as L, except the third assumption (M) is the percentage that repeated once that you expect to repeat a second time, and the fourth (N) the percentage that repeated twice that you expect to continue to repurchase. In the model, 70 percent are expected to repeat twice, and 80 percent three and more times. Obviously, these repeat rates determine whether your brand will be a success or failure, but marketing has little control over them. The function of marketing is to get people to try the product. If they purchase it once and then don't buy again, it usually is the fault of the service itself, not the marketing effort. (You can sometimes induce a buyer to repurchase by offering a special price, excellent customer service, or some other type of marketing incentive, but convincing a person who is dissatisfied with the trial or first purchase to buy again is difficult.) Measuring repeat purchase rates not only provides you with a strong indication of the level of future sales but also tells you whether your service lives up to the promise made for it in your marketing campaign.

Column O in this section is titled "New triers," and the numbers shown are picked up from the first section of the model. Column P is titled "First repeat," and the numbers shown are calculated by multiplying the number of new triers

Figure 5-2. Setting market objectives: repeat purchasing plan 1.

		Assumptions
K. Average Repeat Purchase Cycle (months)		2
L. Percentage Triers Repeat Once		50%
M. Percentage Triers Repeat Twice		70%
N. Percentage Repeat Twice Repeat 3X+		80%

Month	O. New Triers	P. First Repeat	Q. Second Repeat	R. Third Repeat	S. Total Repeat	T. Total Transactions	U. Repeat % Total Transactions
0	0				0	0	
1	38	0			0	38	
2	30	19	0		0	30	
3	63	15	0	0	19	81	
4	45	31	13	0	15	60	
5	53	23	11	0	44	97	
6	60	26	22	11	33	93	
7	68	30	16	8	59	126	
8	68	34	18	26	54	122	
9	68	34	21	19	78	146	
10	68	34	24	35	74	142	
11	68	34	24	32	93	160	
12	68	34	24	32	90	157	
Total	693	279	148	132	558	1,251	44.64%

Figure 5-3. Setting market objectives: repeat purchasing plan 2.

		Assumptions			Assumptions		
V. Average Repeat Purchase Cycle (months)		2		X. Percentage Triers Repeat Twice	70%		
W. Percentage Triers Repeat Once		55%		Y. Percentage Repeat Twice Repeat 3X +	80%		

Month	Z. New Triers	AA. First Repeat	BB. Second Repeat	CC. Third Repeat	DD. Total Repeat	EE. Total Transactions	FF. Repeat % Total Transactions Month
0	0				0	0	
1	45	0			0	45	
2	60	0	0		0	60	
3	150	25	0	0	25	175	
4	90	33	0	0	33	123	
5	105	83	17	0	100	205	
6	96	49	23	0	73	169	
7	108	58	58	14	129	237	
8	108	53	35	18	106	214	
9	54	59	40	57	157	211	
10	54	59	37	43	139	193	
11	54	30	42	78	149	203	
12	54	30	42	64	135	189	
Total	978	479	293	274	1,046	2,024	51.67

by the percentage indicated for assumption "L. Percentage triers repeat once (%)." This rate of 50 percent is multiplied by the thirty-eight new triers shown in column O for the first month. The answer of 19 (38 times .50) is inserted in the third month of column P because the purchase cycle is two months. To calculate the second and third and more repeats, the rates for assumptions M and N are used. Total repeats during the first year are 558; this figure is added to the 693 new triers to arrive at 1,251 total transactions. Total repeat transactions as a percentage of total transactions is 44 percent, as shown in column U. This would usually be considered unacceptable after a major marketing effort. What good does it do you to spend lots of marketing money to induce trial and then have less than 50 percent repeat?

As shown in section three (Figure 5-3), plan 2 improves repeat purchases as a percentage of total purchases or transactions to over 50 percent, as shown in column FF, by increasing the percentage triers that repeat once from the 50 percent used in plan 1, to 55 percent as shown in assumption W. Once again, just a slight increase in one of your objectives or assumptions can have a dramatic effect. A 50 percent total repeat rate is not excitingly high, but combined with the minor improvements made in plan 2 in section 1, total transactions increase from 1,251 in plan 1 (column T) to 2,024 (column EE).

Unit and Dollar Volume

Sections four and five (Figures 5-4 and 5-5) multiply the number of transactions from Sections two and three by the number of units purchased and the price per unit to arrive at total sales in units and dollars. Three assumptions are used. As shown in plan 1 (Figure 5-4), the first assumption is "GG. Average number of units trial transaction." The number 1.1 is used. This means that most buyers are expected to only purchase one unit, but a few will buy several, resulting in an average of 1.1. The second assumption is "HH. Average number units repeat transactions." The number 1.3 is shown. A higher number is used on repeat business on the theory that the customer is now more familiar with the product and that some

Figure 5-4. Setting market objectives: unit and dollar volume plan 1.

	Assumptions		Assumptions
GG. Average Number Units Trial Transaction	1.10	II. Manufacturer's Price Per Unit	$500
HH. Average Number Units Repeat Transaction	1.30		

	Units			Dollars		
Month	JJ. Trial	KK. Repeat	LL. Total	MM. Trial	NN. Repeat	OO. Total
0	0	0	0	0	0	0
1	41	0	41	20,625	0	20,625
2	33	0	33	16,500	0	16,500
3	69	24	93	34,375	12,188	46,563
4	50	20	69	24,750	9,750	34,500
5	58	58	115	28,875	28,844	57,719
6	66	43	109	33,000	21,450	54,450
7	74	76	150	37,125	38,106	75,231
8	74	70	145	37,125	35,198	72,323
9	74	101	176	37,125	50,716	87,841
10	74	96	171	37,125	48,146	85,271
11	74	121	195	37,125	60,317	97,442
12	74	117	191	37,125	58,260	95,385
Total	762	726	1,488	380,875	362,974	743,849

customers are likely to purchase higher quantities. The third assumption is "II. Manufacturer's price per unit." The price indicated is $500. To arrive at total units, the model multiplies the average number of units purchased as shown in the first two assumptions by the number of transactions from sections two and three. To calculate total dollars, the model multiplies total units by the price shown in the third assumption.

Plan 2, as shown in Figure 5-5, increases the expected units per purchase on the trial transaction from 1.1 (plan 1) to 1.2 and on repeat business from 1.3 (plan 1) to 1.4. The minor improvements made in plan 2 compared to plan 1 in this section as well as the previous ones result in a 77 percent increase in total estimated dollar volume. Total dollar volume for plan 1 is $743,849, as shown in column 00 in section four; for plan 2 it is $1,381,821, as shown in column XX in section five.

Share of Market

The last two sections of the model, six and seven (Figures 5-6 and 5-7), compute the market share for the two plans. There are three assumptions. The first for plan 1 is "YY. Average retail selling price." In the last two sections, the manufacturer's selling price to the trade of $500 was used to calculate total revenues. When you calculate market share, you normally use the price to the end user; therefore, the price of $650 has been inserted into the model. This is the price the trade charges the end user. If your company sells directly to the end user, you would use the same price to calculate both revenues and share. The second assumption is "ZZ. Total market in units," and the third is "AB. Total market in dollars." These two assumptions refer to the total expected annual sales in units and dollars by the company and its competitors of the type of product or service the company sells. In the model, the size in units is 100,000—and in dollars, $70,000,000.

To calculate monthly unit market share as shown in column HH, the model takes the monthly sales in units from section four (Figure 5-4) and divides it by monthly total volume (assumption ZZ divided by 12). To obtain monthly dollar share

Figure 5-5. Setting market objectives: unit and dollar volume plan 2.

	Assumptions		Assumptions
PP. Average Number Units Trial Transaction	1.20	RR. Manufacturer's Price Per Unit	$500
QQ. Average Number Units Repeat Transaction	1.40		

Month	Units			Dollars		
	SS. Trial	TT. Repeat	UU. Total	VV. Trial	WW. Repeat	XX. Total
0	0	0	0	0	0	0
1	54	0	54	27,000	0	27,000
2	72	0	72	36,000	0	36,000
3	180	35	215	90,000	17,325	107,325
4	108	46	154	54,000	23,100	77,100
5	126	140	266	63,000	69,878	132,878
6	115	102	217	57,600	50,820	108,420
7	130	181	311	64,800	90,552	155,352
8	130	148	278	64,800	74,151	138,951
9	65	220	285	32,400	109,979	142,379
10	65	194	259	32,400	97,205	129,605
11	65	209	274	32,400	104,615	137,015
12	65	189	254	32,400	94,396	126,796
Total	1,174	1,464	2,638	586,800	732,021	1,318,821

Figure 5-6. Setting market objectives: share of market plan 1.

		Assumptions
YY.	Average Retail Selling Price	$650
ZZ.	Total Market in Units	100,000
AB.	Total Market in Dollars	$70,000,000

Month	HH. Unit Share Market (%)	II. Dollar Share Market (%)
0	0.00	0.00
1	0.50	0.46
2	0.40	0.37
3	1.12	1.04
4	0.83	0.77
5	1.39	1.29
6	1.31	1.21
7	1.81	1.68
8	1.74	1.61
9	2.11	1.96
10	2.05	1.90
11	2.34	2.17
12	2.29	2.13

as shown in column II, the model takes monthly unit sales, also from section four, multiplies it by the price shown in assumption YY, and divides the answer by total monthly dollar volume (assumption AB divided by 12). If you are in a seasonal business, you would not divide total volume by 12; instead, you would make the necessary adjustments to reflect the seasonality of the market.

The monthly market share for the business used in the model reaches a high of 2.34 percent in units and 2.17 percent in dollars. The fact that this business has a lower share in dollars than in units means that its selling price is below the average for the market. Although the value of the assumptions for plan 2 as shown in section seven (Figure 5-7) are the same as for plan 1 in section six (Figure 5-6), market share is approximately 50 percent higher due to the improvements made in plan 2.

Figure 5-7. Setting market objectives: share of market plan 2.

		Assumptions
AC.	Average Retail Selling Price	$650
AD.	Total Market in Units	100,000
AE.	Total Market in Dollars	$70,000,000

Month	*HH. Unit Share Market (%)*	*II. Dollar Share Market (%)*
0	0.00	0.00
1	0.65	0.60
2	0.86	0.80
3	2.58	2.39
4	1.85	1.72
5	3.19	2.96
6	2.60	2.42
7	3.73	3.46
8	3.33	3.10
9	3.42	3.17
10	3.11	2.89
11	3.29	3.05
12	3.04	2.83

When using a "what if" model like the one shown, you can keep making changes in the assumptions you can control until you obtain the desired volume and share figures. Then when you write your marketing plan, you insert as your marketing objectives the level of the various assumptions and include marketing strategies and plans to reach them. If you believe you cannot develop strategies and plans to reach these objectives, then you have to go back to the model and change the assumptions to levels you can reach.

Section III

Marketing Communications Plan

6

Creative Strategy

As stated in the Introduction, the marketing communications plan consists of three separate plans: the advertising plan, the sales promotion plan, and the public relations plan. This chapter is the first of three on advertising. Advertising is divided into four parts as shown in Figure 6-1. The creative strategy, which contains your selling message, is discussed in this chapter. The media strategy and the media plan (how you plan to communicate your selling message to the target audience) are covered in Chapter 7. The creative plan, which is the execution of the creative strategy or the advertisements themselves, is examined in Chapter 8.

For communications people, the creative strategy is probably the most important segment of the marketing plan. Your advertising may entertain. It may be remembered. But if it doesn't induce the target audience to try the brand, what good is it?

Some years ago, Piels beer ran a series of very mod animated TV commercials. The client had high expectations. The commercials had been researched, using a cross section of the population as an audience, and the survey indicated that the commercials were very entertaining. The only problem was that the longer the client ran the commercials, the faster sales decreased. The commercials were researched again, but this time the audience consisted of heavy beer drinkers. (The consumption rate of many mass-marketed consumer products is heavily skewed. The norm is that 20 percent of the population consumes 80 percent of the volume. Beer is even more highly skewed, with 10 percent of the population accounting for 90

Figure 6-1. Components of the advertising plan.

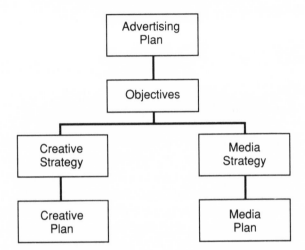

percent of the volume.) These heavy beer drinkers are primarily blue-collar males. When the commercials were shown to this audience, completely different remarks surfaced. The men thought that the highly sophisticated animated commercials were effeminate, and they were turned off by the presentation.

A more recent example is light beer. The first light beer was marketed by Gablingers. They said, Drink our light beer and you will save calories. That's not a bad positioning against the 90 percent that drink 10 percent of the beer. But is the heavy beer drinker interested in saving calories? No. It was not until Philip Morris bought Miller Brewing and introduced Miller Lite with the selling message "Tastes great; less filling," that light beer sales took off. What did the heavy beer drinker want in a light beer? The ability to get six bottles in the gut without feeling bloated. It's no wonder Miller Lite is first in light-beer market share. And these are not isolated examples of misdirected advertising. You see examples of it every day.

The best way to prevent a complete waste of your communications dollar is to prepare a precise and definitive creative strategy and have it approved by both client and agency before any creative work is started. The creative strategy should consist of four parts:

1. Target audience
2. Positioning
3. Copy platform
4. Tone and execution

Figure 6-2 provides an example of a creative strategy. The first section, titled "Whom to Sell," describes the target audience. The second section, "How to Sell," is the positioning statement. The third section, "What to Sell," is similar to a copy platform. A copy platform contains the selling message. The fourth section, "Way to Sell," describes the tone and execution. This creative strategy is long and detailed but serves as a good example of the facts and rationale needed. Normally the creative strategy should be stated in about half a page with the support information in the fact book.

Target Audience

The *target audience* is made up of your heavy users, the people to whom you direct your advertising. It can be defined by demographics, such as age, income, education, and family size. It can also include psychographics, which are life-styles or personalities. A soft drink client and its advertising agency conducted a survey to see if there was any correlation between the consumption of various soft drinks and life-style. The results indicated that different groups of consumers preferred different flavors. The client and agency then developed advertising that was directed at not only the largest demographic group but the most likely customers on the basis of life-style as well. Figure 6-2 is an example of a creative strategy that uses life-styles to help define the target audience.

For target audience descriptions, industrial advertisers generally use the Standard Industrial Classifications (SIC) numbers that have been assigned by the federal government for all jobs in industry. The benefit of using SIC numbers is that the circulation figures for all major industrial magazines are broken down by SIC number. If your target audience SIC numbers are 10030 and 20061, then you look for the magazines that deliver the largest concentration for these classifications.

(text continues on page 80)

Figure 6-2. Creative strategy for Brand X (a line of soft drinks in various flavors).

A. *Whom to Sell:*

The "socially concerned" market segment, defined as follows:
* Upper-middle-income housewives ($30,000+)
* 19–34 years old with children
* Somewhat insecure and self-conscious
* Care a great deal about what others think of them
* Want to be well liked, popular, and approved of by peers
* Rather conventional, not seeking recognition or status in sophisticated society

Rationale:

1. "Socially concerned" persons drink flavors at a disproportionately higher level than the other two major segments of the population, as shown below:

	Segment A Morally Concerned	Segment B Socially Concerned	Segment C Pleasure Concerned
Percentage of population	35	23	24 ·
Root Beer			
Consumption	33	20	27
Index	94	87	112
Lemon–Lime			
Consumption	36	26	20
Index	103	113	83
Cola			
Consumption	36	24	23
Index	103	104	96
Orange			
Consumption	33	26	17
Index	94	113	71
Other Fruit			
Consumption	29	32	20
Index	83	140	83

2. Housewives (19–34 years) with young children are the recommended target audience because:
   a. The housewife is the primary purchasing agent of soft drinks. In the case of colas, the female head of the

household decides on the brand 84 percent of the time; however, she is influenced by other members of the family 56 percent of the time.

b. Younger housewives have younger children who drink flavors at home. Older children are better prospects for vending machine sales, where Brand X does poorly.

c. Families with young children also have an above-average index (111–128) for total soft drink consumption. Children, particularly preschoolers, are not only highly vocal in their preferences at home but have the opportunity to influence soft drink purchase at point of sale. (Children under age 6 are present in their families' shopping units 32 percent of the time.)

d. The brand will not be positioned directly against children, since if it were considered a children's drink, consumption among adults would be limited. In addition, the brand will not be positioned directly against teenagers, since Brand X flavors would be competing against Coke and Pepsi with their $100 + million budget versus our national budget of approximately $10 million.

3. The "socially concerned" segment contains a high proportion (50 percent) of upper-middle-income ($30,000 +) families. Since they appear to be the primary consumers of flavored soft drinks and since the brand is premium priced, this portion of the market is recommended as the target audience. If the brand were directed against the upper-income market segment, the brand's premium price would possibly be more acceptable, but the amount of flavored soda consumed by the upper-income market segment is too small.

B. *How to Sell:*
Against flavor price brands.

Rationale
1. No national flavor lines that are competitive with Brand X flavors are sold in food stores.
2. Flavor price brands account for 76 percent of total sales of flavored soda in food stores and price brands are growing at a rapid rate, estimated at 20 percent growth per year.

(continues)

Figure 6-2. Continued.

C. *What to Sell:*
   Primary Buying Incentive
   Every Brand X flavor has a fresh, natural taste.
   Secondary Buying Incentive
   Brand X quality costs only a little more than low-quality brands.
   Major Selling Line
   Brand X flavors are so fresh you practically have to peel them.

   Support
   1. Brand X flavors contain the highest-quality ingredients and truest-tasting flavors in the industry.
   2. The buying incentive "fresh satisfying taste" received the highest rating as a desirable attribute from "socially concerned" respondents (as compared with other segments).

D. *Way to Sell:*
   The overall tone and execution should set the brand apart as the quality product in the industry.

Positioning

The second part of the creative strategy is called *positioning*. It defines where you want to place your product or service relative to the competition as well as in the minds of the target audience. Do you want to position the brand like a Neiman-Marcus (sophisticated, high quality, fashion conscious) or like a Sears (good value, dependable, middle-America appeal)? Are you a discounter like K-mart or Target or top of the line like Mercedes Benz? Are you a Hertz or an Avis? Are you an IBM or a Dell Computer?

Mistakes in positioning can be very critical. For years Sears was known as the store for middle America. Then, in about 1973, in an attempt to expand its market, Sears went into fashion advertising. The effort bombed. Not only were higher-income people unreceptive to the new positioning, the store's profile became diffused. The result was a loss of many previous customers.

Currently, Sears is trying to reposition the chain as a discounter. It has changed from having periodic sales to "everyday low prices." The problem is that Sears is still higher in price in many categories than the specialty discounters like Home Depot.

Avis took advantage of America's love for the underdog. By positioning itself as number two and trying harder, it significantly narrowed the sales gap between itself and the leader, Hertz. Today, Compaq Computer is trying the same approach in the computer industry.

Proper positioning should give your product or service a personality. If your brand doesn't stand for something, then the brand name becomes just a handle or, simply, just a brand name. Volkswagen used to stand for the ugly little "bug." It was almost a status symbol. Today Volkswagens come in all sizes, shapes, and price levels. The brand name has become diffused. When Volkswagen stood for the bug, its market share among foreign cars in this country was 35 percent; by 1979 it had dropped to 12 percent. Although the diversification of Volkswagen's line may not have been the sole reason for this decline, it very likely played a role.

Another example is Scott. Does Scott stand for toilet tissue, paper towels, or facial tissue? Procter & Gamble never makes this mistake. Charmin (P&G) is toilet tissue. Bounty (P&G) is paper towels. Scott used to be number one in both toilet tissue and paper towels; now the P&G brands are. The fact that each brand name stands for a specific product may have helped account for P&G's success.

Marlboro, American Airlines, IBM, General Electric, Budweiser, and Crest all have unique personalities or brand images—and each one is the sales leader in its industry.

Copy Platform

In preparing the third part of the creative strategy, the copy platform, you should enlist the assistance of your advertising agency or in-house creative people. (Actually, if you have an advertising agency, it should help you prepare the complete creative strategy. In fact, it should assist in developing your entire marketing plan.)

The first part of the copy platform is the basic selling line.

This is a statement of the major benefit of your product or service, made in as few words as possible and in a unique way. Examples you should be familiar with are:

> Does she or doesn't she?
> This Bud's for you.
> We bring good things to life.
> The ultimate driving machine.
> Tastes great, less filling.
> The heartbeat of America.
> Don't leave home without it.
> Fly the friendly skies.

The basic selling line does not have to be printed or spoken. In introducing its personal computer, IBM used a Charlie Chaplin look-alike to personify the needs of a small business and to demonstrate how the IBM PC could solve many of its problems. All cigarettes taste basically the same, but the machismo of the Marlboro cowboy has made the brand number one in world market share for at least the last twenty years. The lonely Maytag repairman says quality more than a hundred words of copy, and the pervasive Eveready bunny pounds home the story of long battery life.

Be sure your basic selling line sells a benefit, not a feature. Black and Decker doesn't sell quarter-inch drill bits. It sells quarter-inch holes. People are interested only in what your product or service can do for them. The public doesn't care whether your product is made of aluminum or steel; it wants to know whether the product will last longer and look better than the competition.

The basic selling line should be included in all advertising. Usually it is your headline. You can change your advertisements periodically, but the same basic selling line should be used for years. "Marlboro Country" and the slogan "Fly the friendly skies of United" have been around for over twenty years. In addition to the basic selling line, two or three secondary lines can also be used to call attention to other benefits of the brand. These are usually the subheads in print advertising and the major copy points in both print and broadcast advertising.

The remaining part of the copy platform consists of the "reason why"—the supportive data that back up your basic and secondary selling lines. Ideally, it should be factual, but not all brands have unique or demonstrable advantages over the competition. If your brand doesn't, consider talking about something no one else is talking about and, in effect, create a benefit. "Reason why" copy is normally the body copy in print advertising and support information in broadcast advertising.

Tone and Execution

The fourth and final part of the creative strategy is *tone and execution*. Normally these reflect your positioning. If you are a discounter, then your execution may be bold and brassy. If you're a quality line, then your tone and execution may be a large, full-color space—you never see IBM use a quarter-page ad. Your execution may include a spokesperson, and the tone may be tongue-in-cheek (Joe Namath), stylish (Cheryl Tiegs), or authoritative (Lee Iacocca). Will humor be used in your advertising? How about testimonials? Case histories?

After the creative strategy is completed and approved by both client and agency, no creative work should ever be reviewed without referring to this document. If the advertising that is being presented doesn't conform to the creative strategy, then something is wrong. Either the creative strategy or the advertising is misdirected. One has to be changed. If you follow this procedure, you cut the chances of having wasteful advertising at least in half.

By checking your advertising against your creative strategy, you are less likely to do ads rather than campaigns. Some advertisers run one ad and then another, with no resemblance between them. If you follow your creative strategy, each ad will contain the basic selling line and reflect the proper positioning. The ads will be directed at your target audience and have the correct tone and execution. Without continuity, your advertising cannot be successful. Continuity will be discussed further in Chapter 8, dealing with the creative plan.

7

Media Strategy and Plan

The media strategy defines how you will use your advertising budget to reach the maximum number of people in your target audience in the most efficient and effective manner. The media plan details the specific media that will be used, during which months, weeks, days, or times, and the size and length of your ads and commercials.

Determining the Budget

Advertisers normally use one of three methods to determine the size of their advertising budget. One is to base advertising expenditures on a percentage of sales. Although this is a common method, it is also the least meaningful. Advertising budget requirements relative to sales volume vary by industry and even for individual products or services within each industry. Advertising as a percentage of sales for the cosmetics industry is two to three times higher than it is for the food industry; the airlines spend at one-third the rate of the food industry but three times the rate of the automobile industry. Within each industry, there is also great variation. *Advertising Age*, in its annual issue devoted to advertising budgets, reveals that there is little relationship between advertising as a percentage of sales among advertisers in the same industry.

The second method for determining the size of your budget is to spend at the same rate relative to market share as the competition. Today it is very easy to track what your competitors are doing in each advertising medium. Various research firms compile advertising expenditures by brand and by company for each medium on a market as well as a national basis. If you are interested in determining competitive advertising weight, contact a representative from each medium for the name of a firm that can issue you a report.

Basing your advertising expenditure on the activity of your competitors makes more sense than using a percentage of sales. Everything else being equal, if your share of market is double that of competitor A, then you should spend at twice that competitor's rate. If competitor A has a 15 percent share and is spending $150,000 and you have a 10 percent share, then your normal rate would be $100,000—but that's just to maintain share. If your strategy is market penetration, then you should consider spending at a much higher rate.

The third and most effective way to determine the size of your advertising budget is to base it on what you want to accomplish. First, you have to decide on your marketing strategy. Are you in a position to attempt market penetration? Or will it be maintenance only? Maybe there are reasons to relinquish share. After you determine your strategies, then you calculate how much advertising will be necessary. The best way to do this involves the use of reach and frequency figures to arrive at the proper advertising weight. To help you determine your answer, use the equation:

$$\text{Reach} \times \text{frequency} = \text{gross number of impressions}$$

If you know two of these factors, you can always calculate the third. *Gross number of impressions* is the easiest to determine, and *reach* is given by readership and listenership research or by your own judgment. That leaves *frequency*, which you have to calculate. To get *frequency* on one side of the equation by itself, just divide both sides by *reach;* the equation reads:

$$\text{Frequency} = \frac{\text{Gross number of impressions}}{\text{Reach}}$$

All three of these factors are always measured against just your target audience. If your target is eighteen- to thirty-four-year-old females, then all figures should be calculated against this segment only. You couldn't care less about the rest of the audience. Also, these factors measure the opportunity to receive your advertising message and do not necessarily mean that everyone will. If you run an ad in a magazine, past research informs that only about 50 percent of the people who read that magazine will actually turn to the page where your ad appears. The same is true with television and radio. For every one hundred sets turned on, only about 50 percent of viewers actually watch or hear your commercial. The other 50 percent are out in the kitchen during the commercials or they are reading, talking, or daydreaming. I will make an adjustment for this later on.

Now for an explanation of the three factors. The *gross number of impressions* is the gross number of times your target has the opportunity of seeing or hearing your ad. If you are using magazines, it is the sum of the circulation of each magazine you are using times the number of times you use it. If your ad appears in three magazines and the same person reads all three, you count that person three times. If you want to use pass-along readers (people who are not the primary receivers of the magazine, such as readership in doctors' offices and pass-along readers in companies) in addition to the circulation, that's fine, but discount the pass-along audience about 50 percent. The reason for this is that pass-along readers rarely spend as much time with the publication as the person who either buys it or receives it free through the mail. For television and radio, the gross number of impressions is the sum of all the times your target has the television or radio on and tuned to the station at the time your commercial comes on.

Reach is the percentage or number of your target that has the opportunity of receiving your message at least once. This is a net figure, and you do not count the same person twice. Reach figures are calculated by research, with Simmons Market Research Bureau, as well as others, determining the unduplicated audience for magazines and A. C. Nielsen doing the same for radio and television. Reach figures are available on almost all major consumer magazines but not industrial magazines. Therefore, industrial advertisers have to estimate this duplication factor. This should not be a major problem, because industrial advertisers should know their trade magazines backward and forward and be able to approximate the reach figure. As you will see later on, a slight miscalculation will not throw off your figures.

Frequency is the average number of times your target has the opportunity of seeing or hearing your ad. Remember, it is an average. That does not mean that everyone will see the ad that many times. Therefore, *reach* (the number you reach at least once) times *frequency* (the average number of times you reach them) equals the *gross number of impressions*.

To give you an actual example, say that your target is adults in households with incomes of $25,000 and over, and your schedule calls for one insertion in *TV Guide* and one in *Seventeen*. Using research, it could be determined that you will reach 10 million people or 30 percent of all U.S. households with incomes of $25,000 and over. This is the number that receive one or both of these two magazines. Research could also tell you that 300,000 of these households subscribe to or buy both magazines. That makes the gross number of impressions 10.3 million (10 million plus 300,000). Using the equation *frequency* equals *gross number of impressions* divided by *reach*, the *frequency* is 1.03. This schedule gives you excellent reach for just one insertion in two magazines, because very few households subscribe to both *TV Guide* and *Seventeen*. The frequency, though, is very low.

The most important fact you should remember about reach and frequency is that you almost always build frequency first and then add reach. Unless you have such a hot product or service that the world is beating down your door to buy, always be sure you have a sufficiently strong frequency against one segment of your target before you spread your reach. If you don't, you will get lost in the bombardment of all advertising and not even be seen or heard. The question then is, what is adequate frequency? Before I answer this, I have to talk to you about exposure. Exposure occurs when the person actually sees or hears your advertising. After I give you a recommendation on the ideal exposure level, I will translate this number back up to frequency.

Effective Exposure

Some researchers say that the ideal exposure level is somewhere between two and three times. Their rationale is that the first time people see a commercial, they say to themselves, "What is it?" or words to that effect. The second time, the mind does not have to concentrate on identifying the message and asks, "What's in it for me or my company?" At this point, some researchers say that the buying decision is made. Others say it takes a third exposure before the buying decision is made. (This is based on the assumption that prospects want the product and also have the money, which is not always the situation. That is why you have to keep advertising to periodically reach the target with an exposure level of 3 and catch these people when they can afford to buy.)

This recommended exposure level of 2 to 3 is supported by other past research. An index of 100 was used as the percentage of people who remembered an advertising message after the first exposure. The index increased to 133 after the second exposure and to 144 after the third exposure. Then something very interesting happened. The index after the fourth exposure was approximately 144. After the fifth, 144. After the sixth, 144. And so on. There does not appear to be any major increase in the percentage of people remembering a commercial after the third exposure.

These findings are supported by several other studies. In *Effective Frequency*, Michael J. Naples* discusses some laboratory experiments undertaken in 1968 by Robert C. Grass† of Du Pont to help better understand the generation-satiation response pattern as it might relate to advertising. Naples quotes Grass from a paper presented at an Advertising Research Foundation conference:

> The work . . . was conducted by the Du Pont Company and Associates for Research Behavior, and it was conducted exclusively with TV commercials. Two criteria of commercial effectiveness were employed. The first of these was a measure of the "attention" or "interest" generated in a subject when he was exposed to a commercial. This measurement

*Effective Frequency: The Relationship Between Frequency and Advertising Effectiveness, (New York: Association of National Advertisers, Inc. 1979).
†"Satiation Effects of Advertising," Advertising Research Foundation, Proceedings of the 14th Annual Conference, New York, October 15, 1968.

was obtained by means of CONPAAD equipment which requires that the subject perform physical work in order to see or hear the commercial. When subjects were exposed to the same commercial again and again on this equipment, a generation-satiation pattern [Figure 7-1] similar to that observed in the work involving simple stimuli was obtained.

. . .

The central question Grass was investigating was how many times to run an advertisement. He did not propose that the generation-satiation studies provided concrete answers to such inquiries but did make the point that the Du Pont Company was searching hard to understand effects of frequency in order to better schedule its advertising. Grass commented:

Figure 7-1. Attention paid to TV commercials vs. exposure frequency. (Reprinted from the Proceedings of the 14th Annual Conference. © 1968 by the Advertising Research Foundation.)

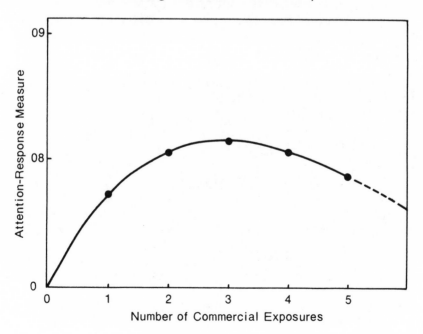

"If this relationship is a true one, then we should expect the point of satiation in attention to coincide with or precede maximization of learned information. Fortunately, we can examine this relationship in the case of the Product A and Product B commercials since these commercials were studied not only from the standpoint of attention (on the CONPAAD equipment) but also from the standpoint of learning in the recall work.

"The curves of both the attention and learning response are superimposed in [Figure 7-2] for the Product A commercial. The two sets of data show that, in accord with the hypothesis we have just outlined, attention increases and maximizes at two exposures, while the amount of learned information increases and maximizes at two or three exposures.

"A similar situation is suggested by the results from the Product B commercial [Figure 7-2] except that the maximization of information level at exactly the fourth exposure must be hypothetical because of the absence of a data point.

"So far, we have confined our attention to communication of facts as a measure of advertising effectiveness, but ads are frequently called on to generate attitudes as well."

Another advertiser's study asked whether there is a positive relationship between frequency of exposure and change in advertising awareness. To examine this question, awareness-switching data were treated as follows:

$$\frac{\text{Total switching in}}{\text{Total switching in } + \text{ total switching out}}$$

is equivalent to

$$\frac{\text{Total becoming aware}}{\text{Total becoming aware } + \text{ total becoming unaware}}$$

Since the total "switching in" (SI) must equal the total "switching out" (SO), by definition, we would

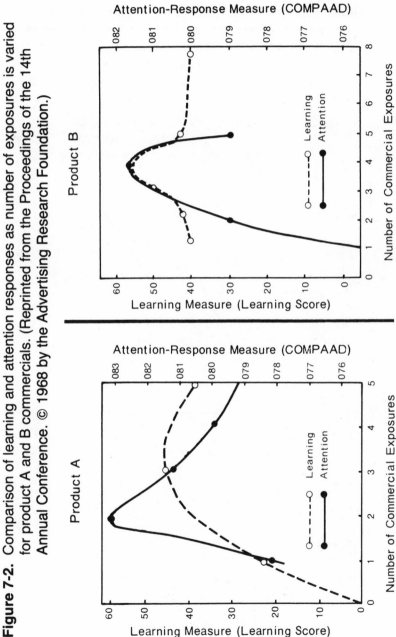

Figure 7-2. Comparison of learning and attention responses as number of exposures is varied for product A and B commercials. (Reprinted from the Proceedings of the 14th Annual Conference. © 1968 by the Advertising Research Foundation.)

expect SI/(SI + SO) to be .50 if advertising exposure had no effect. When the thirty-eight brands were averaged and looked at in this way, the results showed a sharp threshold effect between one exposure and two exposures, but at least three exposures were necessary in a four-week period to give the advertised brands a competitive advantage. This is shown in [Figure 7-3]. The full response function that

Figure 7-3. Switch-in/total switching ration vs. exposure frequency. (*Source:* Michael J. Naples, *Effective Frequency.* Association of National Advertisers, Inc., 1979.)

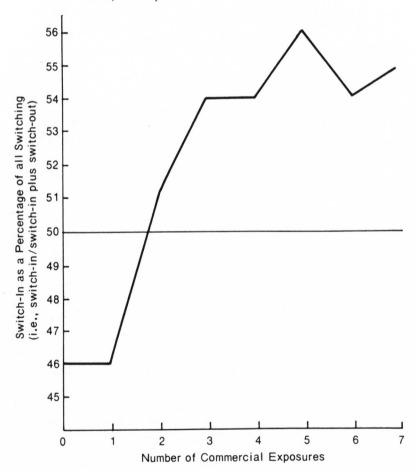

emerged (up to seven exposures to brand advertising over a four-week period) clearly highlighted the advantage of frequency over single-exposure reach.

The research in this chapter may seem dated. Actually this type of research on ideal exposure was conducted many years earlier than the references made here. Nobody believed it except the researchers. How could ideal exposure peak so early? everyone asked. They did the research again and obtained basically the same results. And again and again. Same results. Today you can go to your library and access more recent studies than those shown in this book. The results are the same.

What Is the Ideal Frequency?

Considering that research indicates that the more effective exposure level is between 2 and 4, I recommend a frequency level between 5 and 10. This is based on the previous statement that only about 50 percent of the audience that has the opportunity of seeing or hearing your ad is actually exposed to it. Some agency people recommend a frequency range between 3 and 10, but I believe 3 or 4 is too low. A frequency level of 3 delivers only an average exposure of 1.5.

Therefore, it is recommended that you select media that will give you the maximum number of total impressions with a 5–10 frequency. This is not a simple task. According to Simmons Research, approximately 50 percent of U.S. households account for approximately 75 percent of all television viewing. The same skew is true for print: 50 percent of the households account for approximately 75 percent of all newspaper and magazine reading. When you have 50 percent of the universe accounting for 75 percent of the audience, it means the remaining 50 percent account for only 25 percent of the audience. It is usually difficult to run a television schedule of relatively heavy impact without getting frequency figures up into the 40–50 range. Such high frequency against any segment of your audience is overkill and a waste of advertising funds.

Figure 7-4 shows the exposure rate of a typical 400 gross

Figure 7-4. Reach and frequency for a prime-time television schedule (400 GRPs).

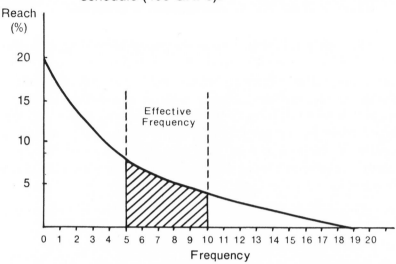

rating point (GRP) television schedule. (Gross rating points are similar to gross number of impressions.) Note that only about half of the total exposures are between 5 and 10. Compare this with Figure 7-5, where the effective exposure level of a desirable schedule is overlaid. The only problem is that, in reality, to increase the reach on effective exposures, you end up getting a high percentage of exposures over 10, which, as previously stated, is overkill.

Reach and frequency figures for broadcast media (television and radio) are usually calculated on a four-week basis. For monthly magazines, the time period is usually one year, and for weeklies, thirteen weeks. In trying to keep a maximum number of advertising impressions within a frequency range of 5–10 over these time periods, you should remember that in practically all cases, you build frequency first, then add reach.

Earlier, I provided an example of a relatively large reach (30 percent) with a very low frequency (1.03) through the insertion of one ad in two magazines. This is not an effective schedule. If you can afford only one insertion per magazine, then you should save your money for some other type of promotional activity. Below are the hypothetical reach and

Figure 7-5. Reach and frequency for actual vs. desirable prime-time television schedule (400 GRPs).

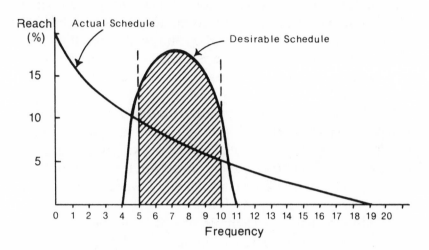

frequency figures for two insertions each in two magazines and a target audience of women over age 18:

> *Gross impressions:*   36,000,000
> *Net reach:*   21,835,000 (31.93 percent)
> *Average frequency:*   1.62

You will note that the reach is approximately the same as for the earlier schedule, but the frequency is now increased to 1.62. This is still too low, however, and it is not until you get up to six insertions in each magazine that you get a frequency over 5.

Television and Radio Schedules

Reach and frequency figures are also available for television and radio schedules. Television will be used as an example, but the same principles apply to radio. A TV schedule that delivers 100 gross rating points (GRPs) a week means that the number of homes you are reaching is the same as the total number of homes in the market. You are not actually reaching every home, but because of duplication, you are reaching the equivalency in number. In essence, gross rating points are the same as gross number of impressions. With 100 GRPs and 100,000 households with TVs in the market, the total times the commercial will theoretically be seen is 100,000. Some homes may see it one time, some three, some five, and so on. Some homes won't see it at all.

Reach figures have been determined through research for the various types of schedules. If you run five spots in prime time (7:30–10:30 P.M.) per week for four weeks, your estimated four-week reach will be very high. If you run the same spots in daytime, your reach will be considerably lower because many homes never watch daytime television.

Continuing with an example of 150 GRPs per week for four weeks, if there are 100,000 homes with TVs in the market and research indicates that your reach is 60 percent, you are reaching 60,000 homes at least once. Your gross number of impressions is 400,000 (100,000 × 4), and dividing your reach (60,000) into the gross number of impressions gives you a frequency of 6.6. Based on the goal of having a frequency between 5 and 10, this type of schedule gives sufficient weight.

If you are using television or radio, you should have a frequency between 5 and 10 every four weeks. This does not mean that you have to be on four straight weeks. In fact, you rarely use radio on a continuous basis. You should use it in flights—that is, be very strong for two to three weeks, then get off completely and come back very strong again. Strong means at least twenty-five spots per week per station and, if you are after the mass market, on a sufficient number of stations to account for at least 75 percent of the total listening audience.

Ideally, television should be used in the same manner—in flights. The problem here is that you can't usually get your spots adjacent to highly rated programs unless you commit yourself to a continuous twenty-six- or thirty-nine-week schedule. If you can get good spot adjacencies in your market on a series of two- or three-week flights, grab them. If not, commit yourself to longer flights in order to obtain the higher ratings.

Newspaper Advertising

Most advertising media people do not use reach and frequency calculations for newspapers. Normally I say that you are not in newspapers unless you run an ad at least twice a month and the size of the ad is large enough to go through the fold or extend more than 50 percent of the depth of the page. This usually means an ad at least 11 inches deep. If the paper is a tabloid, then the ad should be a full page.

If you are currently running one-quarter page ads on a weekly basis, I suggest you consider doubling the size and scheduling them every other week. Some advertisers, like restaurants, are located in a special section of the newspaper, and if you are in their lucky situation, then the above size requirements do not apply. You can usually get readership with a much smaller ad.

Choosing the Medium

Now that you understand reach and frequency, you are in a position to determine which advertising medium will be the most effective for the target audience you detailed in the first section of your creative strategy. If the demographics of your target audience indicate that it is composed of medium to heavy television viewers and your product or service sales story lends itself to an audiovisual presentation, then develop a television schedule that has adequate frequency and reach and calculate its costs. Next comes the question of whether you can afford it. When the total cost is too high, don't make the mistake of cutting back the proposed schedule. Rather, examine other media to see if there isn't one in which you can be dominant, stay within your budget, and still tell your story dramatically. If there isn't, don't advertise. Never use an advertising medium unless you can be dominant, and never add a second medium until you are dominant in the first.

Whenever one of your major marketing strategies is to increase market share, you usually have to back it up with a substantial communications budget for advertising and sales promotion. If funds are not available to be a heavy promoter, then you have to change your strategy. Every segment of the marketing plan relates directly back to your strategic plan and marketing plan objectives.

Determining Length or Size

Sixty seconds is the preferred length for radio commercials. It is usually difficult to get your story across with audio in only thirty seconds. In addition, thirty-second radio commercials usually cost 85 percent of what a sixty-second commercial costs. Why not buy double the time for only 15 percent more?

On television, the opposite is true. Here the preferred length is thirty seconds. There are three reasons. One is that sixty-second commercial time is normally not available during prime time. Second, most thirty-second TV commercials obtain higher recall scores than their sixty-second counterparts. It's surprising, but true. Third, there is no financial savings per second in buying sixty seconds compared to thirty seconds. A sixty-second commercial usually costs exactly twice what the thirty-second spot costs. This does not mean you should overlook the ten-second commercial—it made Hawaiian Punch number one in its category. If you have a short story to tell and insufficient funds to get adequate reach and frequency with thirties, ten-second spots could be your answer.

In magazine advertising, if you are interested in maximum readers per dollar, you would do best with less than full-page ads. Furthermore, one-page ads usually get more readers per dollar than two-page ads. Rarely, however, should your objective be readers per dollar, but rather the ability of the ad to register in the minds of the prospects a strong desire to buy or act. This is called *impact*.

According to one study, the impact of a two-page ad is 225–240 percent greater than the impact of a one-page ad, and a one-page ad scores approximately the same increase over a half-page ad. So if impact is your objective, you will receive more for your dollar with two-page than with one-page ads, and more with one-page than with less-than-full-page ads. Therefore, after you have sufficient money for adequate frequency and reach, you should give serious thought to two-page spreads.

You have to be careful when you run ads smaller than a full page. Many people judge the quality of a product or service by the size of the ad. You probably have seen the little ads in newspapers and magazines that proclaim how you can make a million dollars. The immediate question is, if these people are so successful, how come they can't afford larger ads? If your competitors are running less than full-page ads, you don't necessarily have a problem if you run the same size ad. However, if your competitors are using one- and two-page ads and you're running less than a page, most likely your prospects will consider your product or service inferior to your competitors'. They'll probably think that your product doesn't sell as much as the competition; otherwise, you could afford a larger ad.

Always use color in advertising when the product or service lends itself to this treatment and you have sufficient funds after establishing adequate reach and frequency. Several research studies have indicated that both readership and impact increase at a much higher rate than the increase in cost. Full or four color is recommended, but two and three color can also be effective. Duotones, or two-color halftones, though, should be carefully considered. To some people, they are irritating to the eye.

In summary, the media strategy includes such information as the target audience, the advertising media to be used, the reach and frequency of the schedule, the size of the ads or length of the commercials, the number of advertising flights, and the total budget.

It is hoped that you will never approve an advertising schedule that does not meet the stated requirement for reach and frequency. You don't have to understand the whole concept of reach and frequency to do this. Just tell your agency or in-house media service that if it doesn't have a frequency between 5 and 10 over the given time periods, then something is wrong. Either the schedule is too light and ineffective or it is too heavy, in which case you're wasting your money on overkill.

The media plan includes all the details of the media strategy. If the media strategy calls for television, then the media plan contains the information on what television stations in what cities, the dates of the flights, the number of spots, and so on. If the media strategy states that print will be used, then the media plan details which magazines or newspapers will be used, for which month, week, or day, the size of the ad, and so on.

8

Creative Plan

$\mathbb{A}$dvertising can do only one thing—and that's to induce the target audience to try your product or service one time. In fact, the fastest way to encounter financial difficulties is to have an effective advertising campaign on a lousy brand. Everyone will try the product once, and by the time you refill the pipeline, there will be no repurchasers. Another fact to remember is that advertising is successful only to the extent that it accomplishes its objective. Your advertising may be hilariously funny, it may even be remembered, but if it does not induce the prospect to purchase the product or service or to remember the brand name, you have a problem.

After you complete your creative strategy and have it approved, prepare your creative plan. Your creative strategy, as discussed in Chapter 6, details your target audience, the positioning of the brand, the copy platform (which is your basic advertising message), and the tone and execution. The creative plan details the advertisements themselves—the TV and radio commercials, magazine ads, newspaper ads, outdoor advertising, direct mail, and any other type of advertising you use.

Most advertising agencies have what they usually refer to as their "creative credo." The most famous is probably Rosser Reeves's "unique selling proposition." Reeves, when he was president of the Ted Bates advertising agency, demanded that all the advertising prepared by his agency contain a unique selling proposition—a statement that makes a person want to purchase the brand, presented in a unique way to break through all the clutter and weight of the competitors' advertising.

Benefit Retention

As an alternative to Reeves's creative credo, this chapter presents my concept of what makes advertising effective. Perhaps it is more expansive. At least, it has more specific requirements. I call it *benefit retention*.

As mentioned earlier, all advertising should offer the buyer a benefit. Your target audience doesn't care about the sales or profits of your company or the welfare of your employees; your prospects are interested in what you can do for them. If you do not offer them a benefit, your advertising may be remembered, but it certainly won't induce anyone to try your brand. Be sure that you highlight benefits and not a feature. Many clients and advertising agencies appear to be confused about the distinction. It's the old story of the sizzle and the steak. An examination of advertising today makes it apparent that many advertisers have forgotten to push the sizzle.

Ideally, your product or service has a specific, real benefit. This makes advertising relatively simple. Basically, all you have to do is get the story across. Procter & Gamble never introduces a brand unless research has proved that it has a definite product advantage over the competition. For products that demand huge investments, such as paper, that advantage may have to be as high as 70 percent. In other words, 70 out of 100 people would have to prefer a Procter & Gamble paper product before it could be put on the market. For brands requiring a smaller investment, a 55 percent advantage may be sufficient.

Creating a Benefit

However, most advertisers that market various products and services offer no real benefit over the competition. If you are in this situation, then you have to *create* a benefit in the minds of the prospective buyer. Whether the employees of one airline are friendlier than those of another is debatable, but United very successfully used the basic selling line "Fly the friendly skies of United" for many years. In fact, a recent research study indicated that this advertising slogan was remembered by more people than any other advertising message being used at that time.

If you blindfold people, very few can tell the difference between one beer and another. If you blindfold people who smoke or have had one alcoholic beverage, most can't even tell the difference between Coca-Cola, 7-Up, and Canada Dry Ginger Ale. This has not kept the various beer and soft-drink advertisers from building extensive brand loyalty through such campaigns as these: "Just for the taste of it," "You got the right one, baby, uh-huh!" and "This Bud's for you." Whether people can tell the difference between Marlboro and other cigarettes with about the same amount of nicotine and tar content is also open to question. Yet Marlboro shot from back-of-the-pack into first place practically overnight with its highly successful Marlboro Man campaign.

Positioning is another device that can be used to create a benefit in the minds of the target audience. Bill Marriott positioned his hotel chain right between Hyatt and Holiday Inn, providing the target audience (business travelers with company expense accounts) with almost as much glamour as Hyatt but considerably more than Holiday Inn, at a price the company controller can approve. American Express positioned its Gold Card, and subsequently its Platinum Card, as the credit card for successful businesspeople; targets paid more for their cards just so they could garner prestige by throwing it down on the counter when checking in at an airline or hotel.

Highlighting benefits in your advertising is a necessity, but if no one remembers your message, what have you accomplished? This is where benefit retention comes in. Four requirements for obtaining maximum retention or memorability in advertising are *simplicity, uniqueness, credibility,* and *longevity.*

Simplicity

Some of you may have witnessed the skit where two people are sent out of the room and a very short news release is read to a third person. Then one of the two people is called back in and the person who just heard the release repeats it from memory. Next, the person remaining outside is brought in and the person who just heard the release repeats it to this last person, who in turn repeats it to the entire group. Usually the audience cannot refrain from laughter, because by now there is little resemblance between the news release that was read to the first person and what the third person is saying. You may also have heard the story about President Coolidge's remarks after attending a two-hour sermon. One of his aides asked the president what the sermon was about. The president replied, "Sin." The aide, somewhat startled by such a terse reply, then asked what the minister said about it. Coolidge said, "He was against it."

Your advertising should be a simple message with only one or two major points to register. However, this does not necessarily mean that the copy has to be short. In fact, in a research study by John T. Fosdick Associates, the largest group of industrial ads with the highest readership scores were those with 200 or more words of body copy. There is nothing wrong with long copy. Just be sure that you have a strong headline or visual to draw the person into the ad and make the copy easy to read. Use 12-point type when you can, but never use smaller than 10-point, and break up the copy with bold subheads.

Art directors go through fads, and one that in my opinion has lasted way too long is reverse copy. Reverse copy is white type on black or dark backgrounds. There is nothing wrong with putting a short headline in reverse copy, even a short subhead, but if you do this with the body copy, it will cut your readership in half. This has been confirmed by several studies. It is difficult for most people to read reverse copy, and when copy is difficult to read, people simply do not read the ad.

Uniqueness

In addition to presenting a simple message, your advertising should be unique. Ideally, if you were to take your logo or brand name off your advertising, the public would still know whose advertising it was. Examples of products that have achieved this recognition are Marlboro, Eveready, Green Giant, Chivas Regal, American Express Travelers Checks, and Miller Lite.

Uniqueness can also be obtained from the manner in which the message is presented. The Fresca TV commercials that were used when the brand was initially introduced had snow falling when people consumed the product. The more Fresca people drank, the more it snowed, and at the end of the commercials, there was a raging blizzard. These commercials were so successful that the brand averaged number two in advertising recall after just ninety days. This meant that Fresca was beating both Coca-Cola and Pepsi.

A home builder on the West Coast once used a three-page newspaper ad to present his twenty-five homes for sale. The builder had a relatively small advertising budget and wanted to sell all twenty-five homes within one year. The agency proposed that approximately 90 percent of the entire budget be spent on the opening weekend. This was the amount of the three-page newspaper ad. At first, the client was dubious about such an unusual strategy, but he eventually agreed with the agency's recommendation. In this market, home builders usually used a half-page ad to introduce their new subdivisions. The largest ad ever used was a single page. This was the reason the agency recommended the three-page spread. The agency thought that the public would be so overwhelmed by such a large ad that people would just have to see how super these homes really were. This format also enabled the agency to blow up a picture of one of the homes across two full pages. The picture measured approximately 30 inches by 15 inches. It was difficult to miss. So many people came out to see the new homes that the police had to be called. All homes were sold within thirty days—and the remaining 10 percent of the budget was never spent.

Humor is another device to add uniqueness to your campaign. Comedians Jerry Stiller and Anne Meara were featured in a commercial that made Blue Nun a top-selling wine. They also worked for Lanier Dictating Equipment and were instrumental in making this brand the market leader. Despite the success of such humorous personalities as Stiller and Meara, Bill Cosby, and even Bo Jackson as presenters of advertising, you have to be very cautious with this approach. It is very difficult to produce humorous advertising that is effective. As John Roberts from the Marsteller advertising agency states, "It is like ballet. Either it is exceedingly good, or it is very bad."

A set of humorous commercials for Alka Seltzer turned out to be nothing more than a headache for the client. Although many people laughed and remembered the commercials, sales did not increase. After considerable research, the client realized that the public does not consider headaches a laughing matter. People enjoyed the commercials when they had a clear head, but when something was pounding between their ears, the advertised brand was not the one they chose when they went to the drugstore.

You're usually better off using light humor, as has been done effectively by Jell-O, Polaroid, and Xerox. Remember, you are selling the *benefit* of the product or service; if people remember only the humor and not the brand name, you are back at ground zero.

Music can be a very effective technique to increase retention. Coca-Cola has used jingles very successfully for years. The Budweiser song is now being played by college bands across the country. What better exposure than to have 70,000 fans hear your beer commercial played by a marching band during halftime of a football game? Animation is still another method of making your ads distinctive. The Hamm's Beer commercials depicting the animals from "The Land of Sky Blue Waters" were so popular that people called the television stations to ask what time the commercials would be on the air. Piels Beer also used animation, but as discussed earlier, the approach backfired.

Several years ago, the California Raisin Board introduced a new form of animation, referred to as claymation, in its beloved talking raisin television commercials. Duracell is using a similar technology with the miniature character using Duracell batteries and outlasting his rivals.

Credibility

The third factor that must be considered to be sure the benefit your brand offers is retained by people is *credibility*. If people don't believe your advertising, they certainly won't try your product or service. False and misleading advertising will also get you in severe trouble with the Federal Trade Commission and various other federal and advertising organizations.

One of the proven methods to establish credibility is the demonstration. If you can illustrate in print or show on television that your product performs as stated, it is difficult for the prospect to question your claim. The demonstration is what made television the number one advertising vehicle, and it is probably the most powerful advertising technique of all.

However, demonstrations are not always possible or plausible. Testimonials can be a good substitute. Third-party endorsement advertising, like public relations, can be extremely effective. For example, two computer ads appeared back to back in a magazine. The first one was a testimonial in which a recent buyer stated that this particular computer system saved his company $50,000. On the following page was another ad with the headline: "From 37,000 feet, a computer story." Which one do you think produced the greatest results? Don't ever come to the conclusion that a testimonial, especially for industrial advertising, is boring copy. The prospect is interested only in the benefit of your brand and, if you can deliver a credible third-party endorsement, you'll have a hardworking advertising campaign.

Using spokespeople is another choice that is available to lend credibility to your story, but this approach is effective only to the degree that the spokesperson has credibility. Frank Perdue, president of Perdue, Inc., and Lee Iacocca, president of Chrysler, do outstanding presentations for their companies. Ideally, your spokesperson should be a recognized expert in your product or service industry, but celebrities can also be effective. For example, Bill Cosby is excellent for Jell-O. The biggest mistake is using talent that is currently endorsing your product plus five or six others in different industries.

When you have the choice between photography and art, always use the photograph. People realize that it is more difficult to exaggerate claims or benefits in photography and therefore give this technique more credence. Photographs are also considered more interesting by the public.

Longevity

The fourth factor for increasing retention is longevity. Many clients kill a campaign or a particular execution of a campaign just about the time the public is beginning to recognize it. This is a bad mistake, but it is understandable how it happens. Usually the client sees an ad two or three times in layout form, one or more times in the mechanical stage, and again when the proofs are completed. Then what is the first thing the client does when he gets the final proof? He pins it up on the wall right next to his desk. He's proud of the ad and rightfully so. Every morning when he walks into his office the first thing he sees is the ad. By the time the public is glancing at the ad for the first time, the client is completely sick of it.

Rosser Reeves, when he was president of the Ted Bates agency, ran the same television commercial for a headache remedy for over ten years. As the story goes, one afternoon Reeves was on his yacht with the client who manufactured this particular headache remedy. The client reminded Reeves that he had been running the same commercial for over ten years and then asked how many people Reeves had in his New York office. Reeves replied that there were slightly over 2,000. Then the client asked, if there were 2,000 people in the Ted Bates New York office and the agency had been running the same commercial for ten years, what were these 2,000 people doing to help him, the client? Reeves, being a very astute marketer, replied that those 2,000 people were constantly keeping the client's people from changing that commercial.

United Airlines has been using the "Fly the friendly skies of United" slogan for over twenty years, and as previously mentioned, this advertising line has been very successful. Another effective campaign, The Marlboro Man, has been around equally as long. Many advertisers stop using a successful campaign, and then after realizing their mistake, try to recover lost ground by reinstituting it. Hamm's Beer stopped using its animated animals from "The Land of Sky Blue Waters" for a number of years. During those years, Hamm's Beer sales declined. Taking the campaign off the air may not have been the only reason, but it could very likely have been one of the major causes. Similarly, Hathaway shirts' man with the eyepatch has returned after several years' absence.

To summarize: Be sure your advertising sells a benefit, not a feature. Increase the retention of your brand's benefit in the minds of the target audience by making the message simple, unique, and credible. Constantly check all your advertising to ensure that it's in agreement with your creative strategy. If an advertising campaign does not reflect the creative strategy, then something is wrong—either the campaign or the strategy—and changes should be made. After the campaign is prepared, let it run. Don't change your campaign until you have determined through research that it is becoming less effective in the minds of your prospects.

9

Public Relations

Public relations is difficult to define. Why do so many Americans think highly of General Electric, Du Pont, Wal-Mart, Merck, McDonald's, and Prudential? No member of the airline industry enjoys such status. Neither do corporations in such industries as railroads, automobiles, public utilities, petroleum, apparel, banking, television, and newspapers. Is it because the former have a higher return on investment? Not really. Are their products or services more glamorous? It's difficult to beat the excitement of flying or the glamour of television. Then how have some corporations won such respect with the public, when so many others evoke, at best, indifference? When you find the answer, put a cap on it and sell it as public relations.

PR Objectives

The dynamics of public relations can be appreciated when you consider that the major objective of most publicly held corporations is to increase the price of stock. If top management can't succeed, the board of directors will seek new people who they believe can. It's true that return on investment and anticipated growth are key factors that influence stock movement, but these two variables don't always explain the price/earnings ratio. Public image could be the answer, but there is more to public relations than just image. Also, the public relations needs of one corporation could be very different from the needs of the next.

As with any other form of communications, the objectives of public relations activities should be determined before plans are developed. These objectives can vary relative to the type of industry, management policies, stage in product life cycle, financial position, government regulations, and status of internal communications. Once again, however, as in all other phases of communications, public relations objectives should reflect and help accomplish the overall corporate objectives of the firm.

Whenever possible, PR objectives should be as direct as selling the product or service. One of the greatest public relations campaigns of all time could have been the confrontations between Billy Martin, when he was manager of the New York Yankees, and then-principal owner of the Yankees, George Steinbrenner. Was it all staged? It certainly produced the desired results. The name calling, the public's never knowing when Billy would be fired, the firings themselves, and the rehirings kept the Yankees as the leading sports story for over two years. Of even greater importance, however, was the fact that the stands were filled to capacity, day after day after day.

Usually, such a close correlation is not possible. One of your objectives may be to give ten presentations to stock exchange analysts and five to investment banking firms or trust and fund managers. This would relate back to your company's desire to increase the price of your stock. Your PR objective could be to place ten articles on one of your products in leading trade publications. It could be to increase the percentage of business leaders or customers that rank your firm the leader in the industry from 20 percent to 45 percent. (This would require research to establish before-and-after scores.) Or your objective could be concerned with internal communications, such as establishing an in-house newsletter or setting up a series of meetings among employees.

Raising employee or distributor morale is another possible objective. When Norton Simon bought Canada Dry, he told his advertising agency, Grey Advertising, to do something to dispel the inferiority complex of the Canada Dry bottlers. They were of the belief they could not compete against Coca-Cola and Pepsi. This was the year that Ann-Margret had completed her successful motorcycle show in Las Vegas and was one of the hottest show business entertainers. Grey, on behalf of its client, commissioned Ann-Margret to host a one-hour television spectacular with Canada Dry as the sponsor. The agency also filmed Ann-Margret in a three-minute commercial to be aired during the show. The commmercial was a blockbuster, shot in Hollywood and containing more special effects than many movies. Subsequently, the Canada Dry bottlers were invited to Acapulco, shown the one-hour spectacular, the three-minute commercial, and given all the details about when they would go on the air. Then Ann-Margret stepped out on stage. No bottler remained seated. They were all standing and yelling their approval.

PR Activities

Public relations activities usually fall within one of four categories: financial PR; government, business, and community relations; product publicity; and internal marketing. Therefore, you should be sure that you have one or two objectives for each of these areas that are important to your business.

Financial PR

Financial PR includes annual and quarterly reports, presentations to financial groups and companies, publicity in financial media, stockholder meetings, and all other activity that should help influence the price of your stock, your ability to float bonds, the rating of your bonds, availability of credit and venture capital, the development of a favorable position on mergers and acquisitions, and all types of stockholder relations.

Details on how to write and prepare an annual report can be found in many books on financial PR. You can also write for copies of annual reports from several companies, including your competitors, and examine them. Select which format you prefer, and then adapt it to your own company's story. Normally, your advertising agency should not get involved in producing your annual report. Agencies usually don't like to produce annual reports, few know how, and they probably would charge more than other firms that specialize in this area. Use your agency to provide marketing expertise and to develop and produce your ads. Use a company that specializes in annual reports to handle this aspect of your operation. There are plenty of them around. Find out who developed the annual reports that you've seen and liked. Also ask two or three of the best printers in your area what firms they would recommend. Keep your annual report easy to read (no reverse copy), and give it a look of quality. Just as with ads, people judge the caliber and reputation of your products and company by the appearance of your report.

In your presentations to financial people, such as investment bankers and fund managers, be well prepared, factual, and precise. They usually want to hear from your president or chief executive officer, so you should arrange the meeting and prepare the material but keep in the background during the presentation or interview. If your president is a poor speaker, it is your responsibility to suggest that he or she go for special speech training. It is your job to protect the president and help him or her make the best possible presentation.

Relative to getting articles on your company published in the financial press, such as *The Wall Street Journal* and *Business Week,* keep in mind that every day or week these newspapers and magazines have to fill hundreds of pages. This does not mean that they are interested in just fillers, but whenever you have legitimate news, never hesitate to contact them. Remember, there is no such thing as "off the record," so if you don't want something printed, don't say it. Be sure all the spokespeople for your corporation are aware of this. Don't interpret this as an excuse to hide any bad news, however. Reputable journalists doublecheck your facts and figures, and if they uncover negatives that you failed to mention, they sometimes include them in their articles in a manner that could give you insomnia.

Government, Business, and Community Relations

Creating a business personality that is admired by government, business, and community leaders is one of the most difficult and nebulous tasks of public relations. As mentioned at the beginning of this chapter, many corporations have tried and failed, whereas others seem to do almost everything right in the eyes of the public. The oil companies will probably regret for years, if not decades, how they tried to con the American people. It is difficult to believe that their posture was orchestrated with input from public relations counsel. Compare their image with the favorable image that General Electric and Wal-Mart project. The only specific advice that can be given on this topic is that PR people should attend all strategy meetings within their company. They should represent the public and review all pending decisions, whether a change in package design, advertising campaign, or pricing. If public relations counsel believes the move would not be in tune with the morality and public spirit of the corporation, then management should postpone any action in this direction.

Years ago, research studies indicated that the type of television program a company chose to sponsor did not have any appreciable effect on inducing the viewer to purchase the sponsor's product or service. However, Mobil's sponsorship of "Masterpiece Theatre" apparently helped that company's image. After a number of years of sponsoring the program, Mobil was ranked by business and community leaders higher than any other oil company on about sixteen qualities. (This was before the 1973 oil embargo, when none of the oil companies had a tainted image.) Years of sponsoring prize fights certainly was a major factor in enabling Gillette to build an insurmountable brand share in the shaving industry. Xerox, IBM, and General Electric have also used television sponsorship, usually of relatively sophisticated programs, to let the public know that they are willing to invest in their images.

Obviously, not every corporation can afford to sponsor network television programs, but opportunities to build an image also exist on a market-by-market or local basis. The point is that businesses have to show the public that they are interested in more than just the bottom line. Magazines, newspapers, and radio can be used by companies to set forth the social doctrines they believe in. Local sponsorship of such activities as athletics, scholarships, and aid to senior citizens, the sick, and the poor are just a few of the many opportunities.

Product Publicity

Concerning product publicity, you should adopt the same press philosophy previously mentioned—that newspapers and magazines, as well as broadcast media, are in constant search for news that will be of interest to their audiences. This is especially true for trade magazines. Remember, one article on your product or service is probably as strong as three or four ads, because editorial copy offers the extremely effective third-party endorsement. You should talk to editors about their interest in your new product innovations, product modifications, unusual applications, new channels of distribution, successful promotions, and anything else you can think of that will make legitimate news.

When you prepare your publicity material, try to include at least one photograph. Newspapers and magazines are always looking for pictures. If you submit an intriguing or informative photo and caption along with your release, many times they will at least print the photo, and you will get some publicity even if they don't print the story.

Internal Marketing

Internal marketing is concerned with how you are going to sell your company to your employees. If you were going to work for an airline, which one would you choose? Probably Delta. If you wanted to get into the entertainment business, which company would be your first choice? Probably Disney. The practices of these two companies are excellent examples of how to sell your company to your employees. It is not surprising that these two companies will also be cited as role models in Chapter 13, on customer relations.

Usually the purpose of any activity to improve internal marketing should be to ensure or increase the upward flow of dialogue within the company. House organs that are used primarily as vehicles for top management to communicate to the employees have proven to be ineffective. They have low readership. However, if the house organ enables employees to state their views and relate their activities to management as well as to other employees, then this public relations activity can be very beneficial. House organs should be edited by middle management and employees, not top management or the public relations department. If top management wants to get a message out, it has other channels that can be used. Put the house organ in the hands of the employees. Sometimes it is the only way they can be heard.

Relative to the desire to increase upward communication, public relations people should not be considered out of order in promoting some type of management by objectives (MBO). MBO is still the most popular form of management. It increases motivation because employees develop their own plans and programs. They even set their own objectives, subject to approval by their superiors. This process ensures upward communication because it requires employees to tell their superiors how they are going to perform their functions or tasks.

If you are in public relations, you should constantly be asking yourself how employee dialogue can be encouraged. As dialogue increases, motivation increases; as motivation increases, productivity increases. In today's economy, anyone that helps increase productivity is accomplishing a very worthwhile objective.

Public relations can be invaluable to any company. Just be sure to set your objectives first so you don't waste time on trivia. P. T. Barnum, the immortal promoter and public relations genius, is reported to have stated that he didn't care what people said about him, just as long as they spelled his name correctly. Don't you buy that today—not for yourself, not for your company. First set your objectives. Be sure they are meaningful. Next, develop your strategies and plans. Then if you reach your goals, you have good PR.

10

Sales Promotion

Unlike public relations, sales promotion is recognized by most marketing personnel, especially in the packaged goods industries, to be important and effective. Procter & Gamble and General Foods each spend over $200 million on this activity each year.

In recent years, even high-ticket items are profiting from sales promotion. One major typewriter manufacturer offered its product at a 50 percent discount for thirty days. Chrysler has used a satisfaction or money-back guarantee. This could have resulted in a rebate of $5,000 to $10,000 per car, but the company's strategy performed as anticipated—fewer than 1 percent of the buyers returned the cars for refunds.

Although giving free samples is probably not feasible with high-priced items, what's wrong with using coupons? An automobile dealer featured a ten-cents-off coupon in his ad. This drew more responses and subsequent sales than any other promotion to date. He followed with a "January White Sale." All his white cars were photographed to look as if they were hanging from a clothesline, and the copy heralded the discounts. Once again, traffic and sales were extraordinary.

It is true that corporations that manufacture industrial goods have not yet understood the power of sales promotion. Just selling very expensive products or services and not having retail outlets is no excuse. Many tactics that work for small-ticket items should also work for industrial products. There have to be more sales promotion opportunities for industrial advertisers than just trade shows. One day an industrial firm is going to steal sales promotion expertise from the consumer products industry and be the talk of the country. Then everyone will say, "Why didn't I think of that?"

The attitude of industrial corporations notwithstanding, the need for sales promotion does not generally have to be sold. Rather, the questions appear to be what type of activity should be scheduled and what it should accomplish. With that in mind, the following pages will be devoted to an overview of various types of sales promotion activities:

- Trade shows
- Sampling
- Coupons
- Sweepstakes and contests
- Price-offs
- Self-liquidator premiums
- Refunds
- Trade allowances
- Point-of-purchase displays
- Product bar codes

First, however, be sure you have an objective for sales promotion. Determine how this activity will fit in with your overall marketing plan and exactly what you want to accomplish. Next, decide whether you are going to use an advertising agency, a sales promotion firm, or in-house talent. Advertising agencies are usually not too adept at handling sales promotion unless they have a group or department that specializes in it. Many agencies do not even want to get involved, and practically all are too expensive. Either find yourself a reputable sales promotion company or perform the function in-house. Remember, though, go first class. If you don't, your brand will convey the image of one in trouble. That you don't need.

Trade Shows

According to the Trade Show Bureau, from 1970 to 1977 an industrial sales call rose in cost from $55 to $97. (In 1990, it was over $259.) The cost of a trade show contact also increased, but only from $38 in 1970 to $142 in 1990.

The bureau also states that 83 percent of a company's trade show prospects are not visited by salespeople within the twelve months following the show. Salespeople in components or materials miss 89 percent of the buying "influentials" that stop by their booths. For companies that sell capital equipment under $5,000, 82 percent of all qualified visitors to their booths are not seen by salespeople; for capital equipment over $5,000, the figure is 79 percent. Whatever the category, there are many prospects you can see and talk to only at a trade show. Following are a few basic factors that the Trade Show Bureau recommends that you consider regarding your exhibit.

- *The audience.* Who are they? What do they buy? What are their positions? What industries do they represent? You need an audience breakdown by job classification, by business area represented, and by geographic location. If your show manager doesn't make such a profile available, you'd better look to your own devices for information. You need to know your audience, or you'll be punching in the dark.

- *Space.* How much space for how many prospects? If your potential audience is twenty people per hour, you'll need a 10-foot by 10-foot space. More prospect potential, more space. It's as simple as that. And you probably know that you'll need two booth staffers for every 10 by 10 space to handle those twenty prospects an hour.

- *Budget.* Since the average cost per visitor reached at a trade show is approximately $142, you can start by budgeting $14,200 for every one hundred prospects you expect to reach, and you'll still be far below what it would cost you to reach these prospects through field sales calls.

- *The objective.* Nearly every company falls down on objectives; in fact, less than 15 percent set goals. They don't establish them; they don't write them down; they don't express their objectives in numbers. You're pretty much lost in directing your collateral services, your booth staffers, and your evaluation process without agreed-upon, written, numerical objectives. They can be stated as $250,000 in sales resulting from the show, or sixty new prospects, or five new dealers, and so on. All levels of management understand this kind of objective.

▪ *The exhibit.* Should it be a one-time rental or modular? Should it be custom or system? What sales support must it provide? What functions must it perform? You had better establish where you're going before you buy a piece of handsome hardware. That handsome hardware may not be adequate. In summary, an exhibit does not precede your planning; it follows from it.

▪ *Identification.* Display your company name and perhaps a subhead telling what you do. You only have ten to fifteen seconds to catch their eye. This may seem obvious, but go to any trade show and you'll see exhibitors who keep their identities a secret, who never seem to want you to know the company behind the product, idea, or demonstration.

▪ *Lighting.* Nothing attracts an audience better than light. A well-illuminated exhibit will draw an audience. Without light, the exhibit seems to sit there. There is no action or life. Make your exhibit dynamic by using light, motion, and sound.

▪ *The focal point.* You knew this one all the time—a center of attraction, a major interest area around which the rest of your exhibit revolves. Good print advertising has a focal point with a good illustration or a good headline. You need one with your exhibit, or else the prospect is tempted to say, "Why bother?"

▪ *Promotion.* This one is not so obvious. You've done all the right things. Your staff is prepared, your demonstrations are ready, but what's wrong? Deep down you know that many prospects in the show audience will have only a few seconds to decide if they will stop at your booth. But what if they had three months? They will have three months if you promote and publicize, using editorials, print advertising, and direct mail. Make the audience aware of your presence at the show long before they walk down that aisle. Over 75 percent have present agendas before arriving at a trade show. Use your preshow promotional expertise to be sure you're included.

▪ *Training.* This sounds rudimentary. You may well have an experienced sales staff as well as upper levels of management attending the show, but will everyone work in concert? Will all your people know your objectives and who the audience is? Unless you bring all your people together formally and explain all, there's going to be some expensive time that will be unproductive and diminish your achievements. Train, educate, meet, and communicate all about the show beforehand.

Sampling

Sampling, or free distribution of the product, is one of the most forceful marketing tools available. Procter & Gamble uses it with practically every new product introduction. However, sampling can be very expensive. If you can find a way to get your product into the hands of trend setters, society leaders, celebrities, leading firms, and the like, it is a considerably less expensive form of sampling, yet very effective.

Coupons

According to A. C. Nielsen, dramatic growth has occurred in coupon distribution over the past two and a half decades. In just twenty-five years, the number of manufacturer coupons distributed annually has grown from 10 billion in 1965 to 267.6 billion in 1989. One of the factors contributing to the industry-wide growth is the increased number of coupons distributed by manufacturers of health and beauty aid products. In 1989, they accounted for 21.7 percent of all coupons.

What many marketing personnel do not know about coupons is that redeemers have higher incomes, larger families, and spend more on groceries than the U.S. averages. According to NPD Research (Floral Park, New York), both coupons and free samples boost trial sales and are especially effective for superior products but not for poor products. Repeat purchases tend to be greater among sampled customers; coupons are more effective in the short term, but over time the balance tips in favor of free samples.

Today, the overwhelming majority of coupons are distributed through freestanding inserts (FSI), usually found in your Sunday newspaper. This medium's share of coupon distribution has continued to climb each year, reaching 79.7 percent in 1989, according to A. C. Nielsen.

The disadvantage of coupons is the explosive growth in their distribution. There are so many coupons in the market-place today that redemption rates have fallen considerably in recent years. Figure 10-1 shows the average redemption rates for various types of coupons for selected years during the period 1977 to 1989 for grocery products; Figure 10-2 shows the same figures for health and beauty aids.

Figure 10-1. Trend in average redemption rate by Media Grocery Products.

	1977	1980	1983	1986	1989
Daily Newspaper					
ROP (Run of Paper)	2.8%	3.1%	2.8%	2.2%	1.6%
CO-OP	3.2	3.4	3.0	2.3	1.3
Sunday Newspaper					
Magazine Supplement	2.4	2.1	2.4	1.5	0.8
FSI	5.3	5.1	4.3	4.0	2.8
Magazines					
On-Page	3.0	2.6	2.4	1.7	1.2
Pop-Up/Insert	5.4	5.6	5.1	4.0	1.7
Direct Mail	10.2	11.6	8.9	6.4	3.7
In/On-Pack					
Regular In-Pack	22.2	18.4	18.3	14.3	13.5
Regular On-Pack	14.8	13.3	12.2	11.9	9.6
In-Pack Cross-Ruff	7.4	6.8	6.4	5.5	3.5
On-Pack Cross-Ruff	4.5	4.4	4.1	5.0	3.5
Instant On-Pack	—	—	24.7	29.5	29.1

Source: NCH Promotional Services.

Figure 10-2. Trend in average redemption rate by Media
Health & Beauty Aids.

	1977	1980	1983	1986	1989
Daily Newspaper					
ROP (Run of Paper)	2.3%	2.0%	1.8%	1.0%	0.3%
CO-OP	2.7	2.5	2.1	0.9	0.5
Sunday Newspaper					
Magazine Supplement	1.8	1.6	1.1	0.5	—
FSI	3.8	3.2	2.8	2.3	1.4
Magazines					
On-Page	2.1	1.4	1.0	0.8	0.4
Pop-Up/Insert	3.7	3.5	3.8	1.9	1.4
Direct Mail	7.4	7.2	7.5	6.0	2.4
In/On-Pack					
Regular In-Pack	9.7	10.3	10.5	8.2	8.0
Regular On-Pack	8.5	11.0	12.3	12.3	8.1
In-Pack Cross-Ruff	—	3.1	3.1	2.5	2.0
On-Pack Cross-Ruff	—	4.2	3.0	2.7	5.6
Instant On-Pack	—	—	29.6	32.9	43.5

Source: NCH Promotional Services.

Sweepstakes and Contests

Because of complex federal and state laws, companies have to
be very careful when running sweepstakes. However, many
companies are making very effective use of this type of promotion. Sweepstakes can build the readership of your ads,
assist in dealer loading (i.e., increasing sales to merchants),
and get trade acceptance if you offer the trade its own sweepstakes. But unless you have a very unusual contest concept or

a specific reason for using this promotional vehicle, it is usually better to direct your effort in another direction. People no longer seem to have the time to spend on answering contests. You also have intricate laws that have to be faced. The trade does not get too excited about contests, and the number of entries is quite small. Only 20 to 25 percent of the population has ever sent in an entry to a contest or sweepstakes, and facsimiles, not proof of purchase, account for over 70 percent of the entries.

Price-Offs

Price-offs, or price packs, are items for which you pass the discounted price directly to the consumer by printing right on your package "ten cents off" or "Buy one, get the second one at half price." Price-offs are necessary to increase consumption among present users, head off competition by taking consumers out of the market, establish purchase patterns after initial trial, and create attention on the shelf. Price-offs mean less profit for you, show only temporary increases in sales, and, if you schedule them too often, may degrade your product. They are also less effective in inducing trial than either coupons or samples.

Self-Liquidator Premiums

A self-liquidator is a product that is purchased in huge quantity and then offered to the public as a premium at the same price you paid for it. Because you buy such a large quantity, you usually can obtain the item for about 50 percent of the regular price, so it can be an excellent bargain for your customers.

Self-liquidators are becoming more popular, which probably means that they are working. Prices normally should be kept low, preferably forty-nine cents or less. Self-liquidators can increase the readership of your advertising, but just a small percentage of total households ever sends for a premium. Redemption is usually less than 1 percent of circulation. What usually makes or breaks this type of promotion is whether it is accepted by the trade. The key factor is whether you end up with special displays.

Refunds

According to a study done by Manufacturer's Marketing Services, Bridgeport, Connecticut, consumers are active participants in cash refund offers. In this promotion, the customer purchases your product and then mails in the label for a cash refund. Like coupon redeemers, households participating in refunds have higher incomes and larger families and spend more on groceries than the U.S. averages, according to an A. C. Nielsen study.

Another advantage of refunds, overlooked by many companies, is that it gives you the mailing list of customers who have purchased your product or service. This provides you with an excellent opportunity to contact them directly at a later time regarding another one of your promotions.

The major problem with refunds, as with coupons, is that there is such a proliferation that it is difficult to stand out from the crowd. Research also indicates that many people just use the coupons or refunds for products that they would normally purchase anyway.

Trade Allowances

A trade allowance means that you are offering your channels of distribution, or the trade, free or discounted merchandise. Examples are one free case when you purchase ten, or one-third discount on all cases bought during a two-week period as long as a special in-store display of the product is put up for one weekend. The theory behind trade allowances is that if you offer the trade a discount, the merchants will pass either all or part of their savings on to the consumer or give the product a special promotion to move all the merchandise they bought at the lower price.

Trade allowances are something that you would like to get by without, but normally that's impossible, especially on the introduction of a new product. In addition, in most grocery stores and drugstores today, you have to pay the retailer for your space on the shelf. If you expect to get display space in supermarkets or drugstores, then set some money aside for the trade. If you don't, you'll find yourself stuck way back in the corner, if not in the back room. If possible, tie your trade allowance into obtaining special display space. A trade allowance is basically a dealer loader, and if you are able to get enough merchandise into the channels, your chances of a display to move the product are greatly increased.

Point-of-Purchase (POP) Displays

Obtaining mass displays in retail outlets appears to be a lost art. It's true that supermarkets today value each square foot so dearly that it is very difficult to get them to allow special displays. Some ingenious advertisers, however, have developed display units that sold so much merchandise that merchants fought over getting them into their stores.

For example, many years ago, Hamm's Beer fabricated a 15-foot bear with skates that rotated on a make-believe ice pond. He held a six-pack of Hamm's in one hand that was lifted high in the air and almost touched the ceiling of the supermarket. The bear was identified with Hamm's because an animated bear, plus many other woodland animals, had been in Hamm's Beer commercials for years.

In order to qualify for the display unit, a supermarket had to stock one hundred cases of Hamm's alongside the unit. Even with this unheard-of requirement, demand for the display was so great that some supermarkets waited up to six months for the unit. Wouldn't you like to have been in Hamm's position?

Is it possible that a consumer advertiser could do something like that today? A study by the Point of Purchase Advertising Institute and Du Pont indicated that two-thirds of every dollar spent in supermarkets is an in-store decision. That means that purchasers select the brand after they enter the store for two out of every three items. Obviously, POP material could be very rewarding to the manufacturer.

If mass displays are not possible, there are many other

ways to get your advertising message close to the point of purchase. Shelf-talkers (i.e., printed material fastened to the shelf that talks about your product), window posters, and small cardboard displays are examples. All you need is an exciting concept and a good trade presentation that will convince the store that your promotion will move the product. Remember, the merchant is as anxious to sell your product or service as you are.

Product Bar Codes

The small area on most products that contains the series of lines in different thicknesses and various numbers that is referred to as a bar code has opened a new world in tracking sales and inventory. As you check out in the grocery store or drugstore, the cashier passes the bar code over an electronic scanner not only to establish the price of the item for insertion into the cash register but to keep track of product movement of all items in the store.

In addition, various companies, in cooperation with the retail stores, have established groups of families within various demographics that are given an identification card that they hand to the cashier when they are checking out. Members of these test groups are given a reward for performing this service, usually a discount on their purchase. Using the information from the bar codes and matching this sales data against the buyer's profile can reveal to retailers and manufacturers who is buying what and how often. Taking this a step further, you can subject the test group to various types of advertising and sales promotion and then record what ad or activity actually moves the most merchandise.

You can also purchase the merchandising service that automatically disperses from the cash register a coupon on your product, which is then handed to the buyer every time he or she purchases a competitive brand. How's that for target marketing!

Section IV

Research Plan

11

Market Research

In the past, many companies have conducted extensive research studies only to discover at the conclusion of the report that the information is meaningless, not projectable, or unproductive. Therefore, the objective of any marketing research project should relate directly to marketing or corporate objectives. As in all the other segments of the marketing plan, research activities can be justified only to the extent that they assist the corporation in meeting its overall objective. If marketing research is viewed in this light, then most misdirected research will be eliminated.

Marketing research is a crucial ingredient of the marketing plan. Every corporation should know the answers to these five questions:

1. Who is the target audience?
2. What do the customers want?
3. What does the competition offer them?
4. What can we offer them?
5. What do they think we offer them?

When I go into corporations on a consulting basis and ask the marketing people on the first day if they know the answers to these questions, invariably they say yes. On subsequent close examination, however, they usually realize that, no, they don't really know the answers. Recently, the marketing people within a division of a major corporation ($3 billion in sales) told me that their target audience was five different industries. After repeated questioning, they concluded that their target should be only three. Then I asked them what people in the three industries should be reached. They could list the various job classifications, but when queried on how each should be ranked or weighed, they concluded that they didn't know.

When I completed my two-day conference with this corporation, the marketing people concluded that, in truth, they did not know the answers to any of the five questions. They had a good idea what some of the answers were but could not back up their replies with any facts.

The Customers' Needs

In determining the answers to the question "What do the customers want?" you are searching for the benefits and not the features. Once again, these benefits should be ranked in order of importance. You may encounter a situation where one segment of the market considers a particular benefit at the top of the list and another segment has an entirely different order of importance.

In industrial marketing, you could have anywhere from five to fifteen people within the same company involved in deciding whether or not to buy your product or service. Here you have to be sure that each of them is looking for the same benefit. You may find that the president is mainly interested in cost efficiency, the purchasing agent in durability, and the actual user in ease of application.

The Competition

After determining what the customer wants, you should ascertain what the competition offers. As mentioned in Chapter 6, one of the best ways to help determine how to position your own product or service is to first examine what the competition is doing. Usually, you do not want to hit the competition head-on, especially if those companies have a larger market share. This is the mistake that General Electric made with its computer business. GE insisted on aiming directly at IBM; as a result, it eventually had to liquidate its computer business unit.

Before Procter & Gamble entered the mouthwash business, it determined through research what customers were looking for and how they ranked each competitor on its ability to deliver each benefit. Listerine, the market leader, ranked highest for each major benefit sought, except one. That was taste. Here it ranked last. The results of the study helped P&G to successfully position Scope as the mouthwash to use if you don't want medicine breath.

What You Offer

The next question is "What can you offer the customer?" If your market is segmented, as in the toothpaste industry, you will have to decide what segment you want to reach. Actually, this decision should be made before the product is designed or developed, to enable you to deliver the benefit sought by the particular market segment. Aqua-fresh succeeded in appealing to two different segments and was the first brand to cut deeply into Crest's market share. Aqua-fresh promises both fluoride for prevention of cavities and bright teeth for people who are socially oriented.

If you have an industrial product and are in an industry where different members of the buying groups within companies are seeking different benefits, you may have to consider separate campaigns for each segment. If presidents are mainly concerned with price, then a campaign with an emphasis on price could be run in those magazines read by top management. If, on the other hand, the users are interested in ease of application, then the trade publications read by these people may need a separate campaign stressing that benefit.

You may find that your product or service does not provide any of the key benefits described by the target audience. If this is the case, you have to consider product modifications or possibly even a completely new product. The standard procedure for Procter & Gamble and other major packaged goods companies is to first find out what the customer wants and then develop a product that fills that need. P&G claims that it never has and never will introduce a product that is not superior to the competition in delivering the basic need for a particular target. It took P&G seven years after it bought Charmin Paper Mills to perfect its bathroom tissue. Only then did it begin its heavy advertising.

It is also possible to make customers believe that only your product or service can deliver a certain benefit even though your brand is identical with the competition. The customers think that only you have it because you were the first to advertise it. Within many product categories, there is little or no difference between competing brands. It is doubtful that many people, when blindfolded, can tell the difference between Coca-Cola and Pepsi, Budweiser and Miller, Campbell and Heinz, Maxwell House and Folgers, and on and on. Remember, after people have had just one alcoholic beverage, very few can tell the difference between Coca-Cola, 7-Up, and Canada Dry Ginger Ale. If you don't believe it, try it sometime at a party. You'll be amazed at the results. If you can convince the public that you alone offer a key benefit, such as Budweiser and Maxwell House have done, it is often very difficult to be dislodged by the competition, even though the competition can deliver the same benefit.

Audience Expectations

The fifth question—"What does the target audience think we offer them?"—is often overlooked by even the most experienced marketing companies. Several years ago, Kool cigarettes positioned its brand as a "cool, refreshing" smoke. The commercial showed a chain being broken to graphically illustrate how you could break away from the "hot cigarette" habit and switch to Kools. Subsequent research revealed, however, that the public had an entirely different understanding of the advertising. The breaking of the chain to them signified how to quit chain-smoking.

You also have to be very careful about trying to change your brand's image or altering how the target audience currently perceives your product or service. If Sears had conducted some sound research on the higher-income segment before launching the fashion advertising campaign mentioned in Chapter 6, then most likely it would have realized that the campaign wouldn't have worked. Recently, I was informed by a representative of a corporation that manufactures a watch known for its ruggedness and low price that his management wanted to reposition the brand as a leader in technology. But would the public believe this, even if it was true? The advice given was to conduct careful research, to get direction on whether such a switch would be possible.

If you can't answer these five questions with assurance, then you should use marketing research to find the answers. It is very difficult, if not impossible, to direct and position your strategies without this information. You do not want to make the same mistake that Sears did.

Of course, marketing research involves much more than just finding the answers to the five questions. Marketing research should be used to help determine the current position of your brand versus the competition relative to market share, distribution, pricing, depth of product line, advertising and sales promotion activity, vertical integration, size of sales force, new product development, and all the other factors involved in the marketing function. The need for and applicability of all this information has already been stressed in previous chapters, so it will not be repeated here. Advertising research is covered as a separate subject in the following chapter.

Gathering the Data

If agreement has been reached on the need for marketing research and if the objectives of obtaining such information have been set, the next question is how to gather the data. The first step is to conduct an extensive investigation to determine what information is currently available. As mentioned earlier, the federal government is by far the best source of information. You may have a little trouble finding the right button to push to get the information you want, but persistence pays off. Start with the closest office of the Department of Commerce. The contact that it gives you might not be the right one; that contact may in turn refer you to someone else. But if you keep trying, you might uncover a lode of marketing statistics on your industry.

In fact, especially in light of the freedom of information legislation, you should be extremely careful about the marketing information you provide the government. It could very easily fall into the hands of your competitors. There have been instances when even such confidential information as a pharmaceutical company's new product development has been given to the competition just because the competitor was smart enough to petition the federal agency for a copy of the report that contained the data. Another example is the Federal Aviation Agency, which, after having been petitioned, gave all the engineering details of a new life raft design to a competitor. The competitor then used this information to build its own prototype, and when bids were made to the first substantial customer, it was the competitor that won the sales contract.

Another excellent source of marketing data, especially for industrial advertisers, is trade associations. Today, practically every industry has a trade group, and one of its primary functions is to be a collector and disperser of information. Trade books and magazines are still other sources you should learn to tap.

Your own company's archives should also be investigated. You may be surprised to find that much of the data you are searching for is right there in front of you. Since we have entered the age of the computer, there is no end to the number of cross-tabulations that can be made or, for that matter, the amount of raw data that can be stored. And don't forget the salespeople. They're out in the market every day and should be familiar with not only what's happening but also what the market wants or needs. Some salespeople have a tendency to slant information to suit their own needs, so watch out for that.

Only after you have examined all the information available from the various sources should you make a decision about whether a special research study is required. Such a study is expensive, so you should weigh all the alternatives.

Benchmark Studies

After you select a research firm, the first type of activity you should consider is a *benchmark study*. In other words, where do you stand today compared to the competition in the minds of your target audience? Basically, this means getting the answers to the five questions posed at the beginning of this chapter. The benchmark study should be conducted among hundreds or even thousands of carefully screened customers and prospects. The size of the random sample will depend on three factors:

1. The percentage of favorable responses
2. The error range that is acceptable
3. The acceptable probability that the error range is reliable

For example, assume that you have no idea of the percentage of favorable responses. Then you should assume that it will be 50 percent. This may necessitate a larger sample, but it assures you of a sufficient base. (Actually, in most research studies, including benchmark surveys, you will be asking more than one question, so it is usually wise to assume that the answer to at least one question will approximate a 50/50 response.) Next, assume that an error range of ±5 percent is acceptable. Finally, let's say you would consider a 95 percent probability O.K. The correct sample size, based on these assumptions, would be approximately 400. If an answer to a question was 30 percent favorable (or unfavorable), then you would have a 95 percent probability that the answer was between 25 percent and 35 percent. If you want to decrease the error range, you have to remember that to cut the error range in half necessitates a sample four times as large. To decrease the error range from ±5.0 percent to ±2.5 percent would mean the sample would have to be increased to approximately 1,600. You can determine the correct sample size for any combination of the above three variables from charts in a statistics book or from any marketing research firm.

In your benchmark study, you may want to get answers to more than just the five questions. For example, you could get a reading on what percentage of the target audience mentions your brand name when asked to name brands in your industry (*brand awareness*); what percentage would buy your brand the next time they are in the market (*desire to buy*); and what, if any, of your advertising message they can recall (*advertising recall*). (Advertising research is discussed in greater detail in the following chapter.)

Your benchmark survey can also address such issues as competitive market share, distribution, pricing, depth of product line, advertising, and sales promotion expenditures, although it is usually less expensive to subscribe to the special studies that concentrate in these areas. Their information will also probably be more accurate, because they use a large sample base. Some of the sources for this type of information were mentioned earlier in the chapter. Your marketing research firm can provide you with a more complete list.

Survey Methods

There are basically three methods of conducting a survey: personal interviews, telephone interviews, and mailed questionnaires. Each one has advantages and disadvantages. The personal interview gives you the opportunity to ask the maximum number of questions; the interviewer can probe or ask follow-up questions; the product can be shown or visuals can be used; the interviewer can record his or her own observations; and there is a greater completion rate of questions and interviews. The disadvantages are cost, time required, and interviewer bias.

The advantages of the telephone survey are their short completion time, their lower cost compared to personal interviews, and the chance to call back if the respondent is busy. The disadvantages are you can only ask a few questions; the person you want may not come to the phone; and you cannot use graphics.

The advantages of the mailed questionnaire are that it provides anonymity; it allows respondents to answer the questions at their leisure; and it is the least costly of the three methods. The disadvantages are the low rate of return of completed questionnaires; the possibility that the returned questionnaires may not be representative of the universe; the lack of opportunity to eliminate any confusion; and the long time needed to get back completed questionnaires.

12

Communications Research

The purpose of communications research is to determine whether your communications activities (advertising, sales promotion, and public relations) are reaching their objectives. Even if your communications budget is only $10,000, it is wiser to spend $1,000 in research to get a fix on whether the other $9,000 is working than to waste the entire $10,000. The major problem with marketing people is that they have a tendency to judge their communications activity, especially advertising, in light of their own preferences and idiosyncrasies rather than the anticipated viewpoint of the target audience.

This is especially true for consumer advertisers. You have to remember that the target for mass consumer products and services is primarily the average man and woman. However, most of the marketing people who approve today's advertising campaigns represent the top 10 percent of the country in education and intelligence. They don't think or act like the public they are trying to reach with their brands. You have to learn to shift gears when you are preparing and critiquing your advertising. You must continually ask yourself, "How will the people in my target audience interpret this? Will they understand it? Is this the best possible way to present to them relative to their life-styles, goals, and needs?"

Even the Federal Trade Commission, when determining whether advertising is misleading, thinks about how the men and women of middle America will react to a particular commercial. If the Commission believes that they will interpret your message in a way that's misleading, you're in trouble. The FTC doesn't care what *you* considered the ad to be saying. In fact, if your lawyer responsible for advertising clearance ever says, "This is what we intended," get yourself a new lawyer.

Industrial advertisers do not normally have such a severe problem with misdirection of their messages. The FTC considers the industrial market more sophisticated than middle America, possessing a greater ability to discern fact from puffery. As a result, the FTC rarely reviews industrial advertising. This does not mean, however, that industrial advertisers don't miss the mark. The usual problem is that the advertising is too technical. It emphasizes features rather than benefits. A common situation is where the industrial advertiser claims the advertising agency copywriter does not have the ability to write the technical body copy. "The writer just doesn't understand my product" is the complaint. Consequently, the client writes the copy, and the only people who can comprehend the message are the company's own technical staff.

If you are writing your own body copy, you're probably making a mistake. If you are a hotshot writer, then join an advertising agency. You'll probably make a lot more money. On the other hand, if you've given the agency ample opportunity to learn all the facts about your product and it still can't write copy directed at the target, then fire the agency.

All the preceding commentary underscores the need for communications research. As stated earlier, most marketers cannot rely on sales records to determine whether their advertising is effective. Their only measurement is their own judgment, which could be misleading, and research. This is not to imply that research is infallible. Research can also be deceptive, but it is an invaluable marketing tool when properly conducted and interpreted. In the following pages, I first discuss advertising research, then sales promotion and public relations research.

Advertising Research

There are basically three types of advertising research: *concept* or *copy testing, pretesting,* and *post-testing.* From your benchmark study, you should have been able to isolate the benefits sought by the target audience for the products or services within your particular industry. You should also now be in a position to select the primary benefit of your brand that you wish to promote. For example, let's say your product is a lemon-lime soft drink. You have written your creative strategy and your agency or in-house operation has come up with two concepts. (Normally, you should start with three to four concepts, but for this illustration, only two will be used.) One concept (A) positions the brand as the coolest refreshment of them all. It has a frosty, freezing taste. The second concept (B) positions the brand as an alternative to cola drinks. It claims a cool, clean taste that is preferred by older teens rather than the sweetness of colas, which should be left to the younger teens.

Concept Testing

You and your agency believe that both concepts offer excellent opportunities. The problem is that you can go with only one, so you decide to subject them both to concept testing to determine which one is the most effective. Your agency prepares a brief series of graphics on each of the two concepts. These are not ads, but rather illustrations of ideas. There are no headlines or body copy. However, you could also test at the same time several different copy lines or phrases. When the art is completed, you set up your sample. This should be drawn from members of your target audience, not the universe at large. Many advertisers have failed to do this, and their data subsequently proved invalid.

The sample size can be modest. Usually you only need about 100 people. The research should be done in person, unless you can mail the graphics to your sample and then interview the respondents on the telephone. What you are looking for is which concept has the greatest appeal. Factors you should consider measuring are interest, believability, meaningfulness, memorability, and the respondents' desire to buy. Ideally, you should have data from past concept testing to provide you with some comparative scores. If this is your first concept test, you will not have your own data bank, but possibly your marketing research firm can supply this type of information.

For the purpose of this illustration, assume that concept A received a higher overall score than concept B. The next step would be to prepare the actual advertising (copy and layout for print, scripts for radio, and storyboards for television). Normally, two to four different campaigns would be prepared, each one an execution of the winning concept. We will discuss two campaigns here. The first campaign features young adults in various activities, such as playing pool and throwing a Frisbee on the beach. When they start drinking the brand (called Frigit), it starts to snow. The more they drink, the more it snows, and at the end of the commercial, it is a raging blizzard. The basic copy line is "The frosty, freezing taste of Frigit. It's a blizzard." (This is similar to the original Fresca campaign that I helped develop.)

The second campaign depicts the brand as so cool that when you pour it from the bottle, you don't need a glass. It forms the shape of a column, just as if it were frozen. The commercials show young adults in various activities, such as drinking Frigit with no glass and balancing it on their shoulders when they are water-skiing. The basic copy line is "The coolest drink in town. It's a freeze!"

Pretesting

Now that the two campaigns have been developed, they can be tested against each other, as well as against past research scores or norms, to determine which one is the most effective. This is called pretesting. If you are using print media, representative ads of each campaign are prepared. They do not have to be completely finished ads. For example, if you are using four-color art, you can use a "C" print, which is similar to a print of a color photograph taken with your own camera, rather than going to the expense of color separations. The ads can be tested several different ways. They can be pasted into a dummy magazine and the participants asked to read or glance through the publication. After they have completed this task, they are asked questions on several subjects, just some of which pertain to your ads. This keeps the reason for the questions a mystery to prevent bias. The sample does not have to be large. One hundred people seeing ad A and 100 seeing ad B is sufficient— but be sure they all qualify as members of the target audience.

Another pretesting method for print is to show the participants a set of six to ten ads, one of which is the ad you are testing. The other ads can be competitors' ads or advertising for unrelated products or services. Ask the participants to rank the ads on such factors as interest, credibility, and their desire to try the product. Then you can ask them open-ended questions, such as "What do you think this ad says? Does the illustration appeal to you? Why? What about the headline?" There are many other techniques that can be used for pretesting a print ad, and you can get this information from your market research firm. The firm will also provide you with all the details on the type of questions that can be asked, sample size, and costs.

If you are using television, then you can *pretest* using rough commercials and the services of a firm, such as Burke Marketing Research, Inc., Cincinnati, Ohio. Rough commercials can be *animatics*, which means the message is done in rough drawings or animation, but not in final form. Or you can use a series of still photographs rather than going to the expense of filming live action.

Burke can arrange to schedule your rough commercial in a particular city. The day before the commercial is to be telecast, the firm will make phone calls to approximately 400 households and ask the adult who is home during the day if he or she will watch the particular television program that is to carry your commercial. All pretesting is done during daytime television hours because there is less variation between rough and finished commercials during this time than during prime-time viewing hours.

The day after the commercial has been aired, the interviewers call back the 400 people to see if they watched the program. Usually about 150 have, and these people are interviewed. *Claimed recall* (the percentage who state they saw the commercial after being prompted by either a reference to the product category or the specific brand name) is measured. For example, the viewer is asked, "While watching program X yesterday morning, did you see a commercial for any laundry starches?" If the answer is yes, the person is asked, "What brand was that?" If the answer is no or an incorrect brand is named, the person is asked, "While watching program X, did you see a commercial for brand Y laundry starch?"

The next measurement is *related recall*, which indicates whether any parts of the sales message, situation, or visual elements can be remembered. This is the important score, because it doesn't do much good if the person remembers your commercial but not the message. Besides, many people say they remember the commercial (claimed recall), even though they don't, because they are just trying to be cooperative or nice to the interviewer.

The respondents are then asked to repeat verbatim the sales message and describe the visuals and any other elements they remember.

The research firm sends you the results of the pretest a few weeks later, along with average test scores for previously tested commercials in your product category.

The pretesting research should determine which execution is superior. You are now in a position to produce your campaign in final form and release it to the media you have selected. After your newspaper or magazine ads have run or your radio or television commercials have been aired, you can test them again, this time in their final form. This is called post-testing.

Post-Testing

The least expensive type of post-testing research is readership or interest studies. Many researchers frown on using readership tests as a measurement of the effectiveness of advertising. It's true that testing the persuasiveness of an ad, or even using awareness or recall techniques, comes closer to revealing whether advertising will influence sales. However, many advertisers simply cannot afford the cost of these more sophisticated types of research studies. Also, readership research can be very revealing if used the correct way. Starch Inra Hooper, Mamaroneck, New York, is the leading proponent of readership research with its well-known Starch reports. The cost is approximately $500 per report.

In a Starch report, you receive three scores for your ad, as well as for all other ads in the magazine being researched. The first score is the percentage of people who can remember seeing your ad. The second score is the percentage of respondents who, in addition to remembering your ad, can also state the name of the advertiser. The third score is the percentage of the respondents who read 50 percent or more of the body copy. When a Starch report is conducted on a particular magazine, the name of the advertiser in each ad is covered up with tape. Interviewers call on 100 people who subscribe to this particular magazine, go through each page with the respondent, and obtain the three scores. Because the sample is quite small, the standard deviation is quite large. This means that the only way to analyze Starch scores is to compare the big swings. Since you receive the scores for all the ads in the magazines, you have the opportunity to compare your own scores with your competitors'. If your ad receives a score of 30, you should not consider it superior to another ad that received a 28. But if you receive a 40 score on your ad and your competitor received only a 20, then you can conclude that you are doing something right or your competitor is doing something wrong.

One of the major advantages of Starch tests is that they can weed out ineffective ads. It is true that an ad can have a high readership score and still not induce readers to try the product, but you can never induce anyone to try your product if people don't first read your ad. If your ad gets a high readership score, you at least know that it is being read. The remaining question is whether it is selling your product.

Starch does not limit itself to just readership reports. Two of several other types of advertising testing the firm performs are *perceptual-meaning studies* (PMS) and *impression studies*. The PMS technique assumes that advertising research must determine not only what advertising does to people but also what people do with advertising. Its objectives are:

- To determine the speed and clarity with which an ad is perceived and communicates the product type and brand name.
- To determine in depth the meaning of the advertisement

to the reader. (This diagnostic information tells whether the things that engaged and impressed the reader are meaningful or not, and why.)

The perception portion of a PMS uses timed exposures to test the ad. The advertisement is shown on a Port-T-Scope, a specially designed electronic tachistoscopic presentation instrument. Each person sees the advertisement first for a brief exposure and then is questioned on recall of product, brand, illustration, copy, and the main idea of the ad. Respondents are then shown the advertisement for a longer interval and asked the questions again. To determine their comprehension of the ad, respondents are shown the advertisement a third time and given a series of open-ended and/or scaled or imagery questions designed to reveal what the ad presentation and message mean to them.

By analyzing how much the person sees during controlled exposures and comparing this to the norms, a PMS can show whether the perception of the ad is good, bad, or indifferent. By analyzing what the ad means to the respondent, a PMS can determine what is aiding communication and what may be hindering it.

The PMS findings are submitted in the form of a written report. Responses are analyzed and presented in four basic areas, with norms for each:

1. Extent of perception of the ad
2. Identification of the product and brand
3. Communication of specific ad content
4. Meaningfulness of the intended message, in terms of reader involvement, perceived meaning, and product orientation

The impression studies channel the reader's thoughts into four general areas:

1. The advertisement as a whole
2. The product, service, or company
3. The illustration
4. The written material

Once readers talk about any one of these areas, the stage is set to carry out the real purpose of this research, which is to have readers express their real reactions to the advertisement. Working from the verbatim reader responses, Starch researchers make a comprehensive analysis of each advertisement studied. Clients are told how many readers reveal positive, neutral, or negative attitudes toward the advertisement as a whole, the illustration, the major copy points, the company, and the product or service. The report also explains how and why readers interacted with the advertisement to produce these attitudes.

Many other methods for post-testing magazine advertising are used by various research firms. The same is true for newspaper advertising. However, there is not as great a demand for newspaper ad research, because most of these advertisers are retail merchants. They usually have the advantage of knowing whether their advertising is effective by just counting the sales of the items featured. What they sometimes don't know, though, is how much more they could have sold if their ads had been more dramatic, eye-catching, persuasive, or unique.

If inquiry cards or coupons are used in your magazine or newspaper advertising, it should be the responsibility of someone in either the advertising or sales department to sort the leads, keep records to be sure that the hot ones are contacted, and decide what criteria will be used to measure results. If there is no way that you can ascertain whether the inquiries are accomplishing some predetermined objective, then it is usually preferable to drop the whole system, including the inquiry cards. However, don't use this rationale as a cop-out. Most of the time a measurement can be established. The claim that the sales force just simply will not report back on the status of the leads sent to them is no excuse. If you encounter this problem, keep going up the chain of command, even to the president, if necessary, until you reach someone who will demand sales force cooperation.

Figure 12-1 is an example of an advertising inquiry analysis form that you might find helpful in developing a procedure to determine whether your sales leads program is profitable. This same type of analysis can also be adapted to your trade shows.

Figure 12-1. Advertising inquiry analysis form. (*Source:* Cochrane Case and Kenneth I. Barash, *Market Problem Solver,* Chilton Book Co., Radnor, Pa., 1976.)

PUBLICATION OR MEDIA _____ SIZE _____ SPECIAL CHARACTERISTICS _____ COST $ _____

LOCATION _____ DATE _____ PRODUCT _____

THEME _____

(1) NUMBER OF WEEKS AFTER APPEARANCE OF AD (lease, show, etc.)	(2) DATE (week) INQUIRIES RECEIVED	(3) NUMBER RECEIVED THIS WEEK	(4) RUNNING TOTAL OF INQUIRIES (cumulative)	(5) COST PER INQUIRY: COST OF AD ÷ COLUMN (4)	(6) NUMBER QUALIFIED LEADS		(7) COST PER QUALIFIED LEAD:COST OF AD ÷ COLUMN (6B)	(8)[7] $ SALES TRACEABLE TO INQUIRY		(9) SALES PER $ OF MEDIA INVESTMENT: COLUMN (8B) ÷COST OF AD
					(A) THIS WEEK	(B) RUNNING TOTAL		(A) THIS WEEK	(B) RUNNING TOTAL	
							COMPUTE EVERY 4 to 6 WEEKS			
1										
2										
3										
4										
5										
6										
7										
8										
9										
10										
11										
12										
13										
14										
15										

Remember, as with every other aspect of marketing, if you don't know whether it is working, don't continue doing it.

A brief commentary on the research results of the Lanier Dictating Equipment advertising that ran in Chicago will serve as an example of how to test a radio campaign. It's also an illustration of what happens when your advertising is powerful and on target. Two radio commercials featuring comedians Jerry Stiller and Anne Meara were developed by Lanier's agency, Marsteller. Before the commercials ran, a telephone research study was conducted to measure the level of brand name awareness, preference for the brand, and advertising recall. Then the commercials were put on the air for six months, followed by another wave of research. After only six months, brand name awareness had increased from 11 percent to 32 percent; preference for the brand had gone from 6 percent to 27 percent; and advertising recall from 3 percent to 55 percent. That is the way to research—and the commercials were obviously the way to advertise.

For post-testing of television commercials, Burke Marketing Research, Inc., is one of the most widely used firms, just as it is for television pretesting. The method the firm uses for post-testing is quite similar to its pretesting format. In post-testing, however, the prospective participants are not alerted the preceding day, either daytime or prime time can be used, and the sample includes more than one city. Claimed recall, related recall, verbatims of the sales message, and descriptions of the situation and visuals are obtained the same way as in pretesting.

The percentage scores on claimed recall and related recall for both methods are based on the total number of homes where someone was actually watching television just before the commercial rather than on the number that had their television sets on. As mentioned in Chapter 7, there can be a big discrepancy between these two figures, because many people leave the room when the set is on or remain in the room but do not watch the set. Burke determines the number actually watching by asking questions about what was shown immediately before and immediately after the commercial. If any participants cannot answer these questions, then they are excluded from the sample. Burke indicates that the audience for commercials can vary anywhere from 35 percent to 95 percent of those homes with sets turned on.

Also of interest is the fact that commercials with the highest related recall do not always obtain the best recall of the sales message. As I've stressed many times already, you advertise to persuade the target audience to try your product or service. Therefore, those commercials that evoke verbatim recall of the sales message are the winners and not necessarily those that obtain just a high recall.

The cost of a Burke post-test, which is called day-after recall (DAR), varies by the Nielsen rating of the program that contains your commercial. Programs with higher ratings have more people watching them, and consequently fewer people have to be called to obtain an adequate sample size. The result is a lower research cost for programs with high ratings, but of course the air time for a commercial costs more during high-rated programs than during lower-rated programs.

One other method of testing television advertising is a unique format that attempts to determine the direct effect on the viewer's desire to buy the product. Participants are invited into a theater for the ostensible purpose of critiquing a movie. Before the viewing, they are asked to fill out a questionnaire on their brand preferences. Next they see the movie, which contains a few commercials, and then are asked for comments. Finally, they are given between ten and twenty-five dollars to spend at the supermarket next door, and a record is made of brands selected. The effectiveness of the television commercials is judged on their ability to persuade the viewers to switch from their original preferences as stated on the questionnaire and buy the advertised brands in the store.

Not all advertisers need to subject their advertising to each step—concept testing, pretesting, and post-testing. Many major advertisers do, however, and when you examine the large range of scores, you can see that it can be very beneficial. If research shows that one of your campaigns delivers a 20 percent recall and another 40 percent, then eliminating the first campaign and going with the second in essence doubles the effectiveness of your media budget. It should also be mentioned that advertisers that pretest receive higher post-test scores than companies that don't.

Evaluating Other Communications Activities

Measuring the effectiveness of a sales promotion activity is much easier than measuring the effectiveness of advertising because there are fewer variables. If your sales promotion involves coupons or premiums, you can count the number of each that are redeemed and compare the results with your original objectives. Trade allowances can be measured by how much merchandise you can load on the trade; contests and sweepstakes can be measured by the number of entrants; and price-offs, by sales before and after the promotion. Once again, the most important aspect of sales promotion activity is to set an objective and to be sure that that objective is going to be meaningful to the success of your product or service. Then measuring whether or not you reach the objective is relatively simple.

On the other hand, measuring the effects of public relations can be as difficult as measuring the effects of advertising, especially if you are concerned with creating a favorable corporate image. This requires periodic research to get a reading from your public on such various qualities as technology, service, community or national spirit, human relations, and business leadership. Some research firms conduct this type of research on a regular basis. One such firm is the Opinion Research Corporation, which conducts what is known as its Executive Caravan Survey on a quarterly basis during the year. (Five hundred top- and middle-management executives are interviewed in their offices to gather data for clients. The clients buy in for specific survey questions and ultimately receive the data they ordered. No one else sees this information.)

Ideally you could track your financial PR by the number of institutions that purchase your stock, by your access to credit or venture capital, and even by the price of your stock. The problem is that there are so many other variables that tracking is usually next to impossible. You are probably better off setting measurable objectives, as defined in Chapter 9.

Product publicity can be measured by the number of articles you get placed in magazines and newspapers and on broadcast media. Internal communications could be tracked by a series of in-house questionnaires, suggestion boxes, periodic question-and-answer meetings with employees, and the turn-over within the company.

There are many excellent research companies throughout the country. You should contact two or three of them and discuss how they would propose measuring your communications activities. Some advertising agencies have excellent research departments. If you have no problem with having the same company that helps execute a plan also measure the results, then enlist the services of your agency's research department. If you believe that one company should execute and another test results, then use an independent research firm. What is most important is to subject your communications activities to some type of research. If you don't, you will have no idea whether your efforts are a success or a failure.

Section V

Customer Relations Plan

13

Customer Relations as Part of Marketing

With my young granddaughter, Kelly Fraser, I recently revisited Stew Leonard's dairy store in Westport, Connecticut. It began as a dairy store, but today it's reputed to be the most profitable grocery store in the country, most likely in the world. Inside the front entrance is a message engraved in a large rock. The heading refers to the store's policy, which consists of two rules. The first rule states that the customer is never wrong. Rule two states that if the customer is wrong, refer back to rule number one. Once inside, we found, among all the customers and merchandise, a musical band with singing milk cartons, a replica of a cow that mooed, an employee dressed like a baby chicken and what I believe was supposed to be an artificial animated dog. The dog played the guitar and sang. There was also a talking hen that lays a "Stew Leonard's egg" upon request.

Kelly's eyes could not have gotten larger. Neither could those of hundreds of other children who were there with their fathers and mothers. Their parents' shopping carts were piled high with groceries; some were even pushing one cart while dragging another that was completely filled. The store is huge. You know the merchandise is fresh, but not only because it moves off the shelves so fast. There is a bottling line for such items as orange juice and lemonade. You see the cartons being filled and then shot down the conveyor belt into the arms of customers. There must have been at least twenty butchers whom you could see through the glass wall behind the meat counters. They had to hustle to keep the shelves full. You could also see the produce people behind their glass wall, pulling fresh merchandise off trucks and carting it to the bins. You would think with such a large crowd, there would be long checkout lines. Not so. There were twenty-five checkout counters. If you purchased a minimum amount of groceries, you were given a free ice cream cone on your way to your car.

You may credit the success of the store to excellent merchandising, as discussed in Chapter 10. But it is more than that. Store personnel meet with customers in an upstairs room most Saturday mornings. The purpose of the meetings is to give the customers an opportunity to tell employees what they don't like about the store. The employees listen and, when the customers' comments make sense, they lead to changes in store layout and in brands carried. All of the employees we encountered were extremely polite and knowledgeable about the complete operation of the store. The animated characters in the store do their number at preset intervals. While Kelly and I were waiting for the singing dog to reappear, I asked an employee walking by how long before the next show. With a big smile, he said, "Seven minutes."

This is called superb customer relations. Compare this experience with your last trip to your grocery store. Many companies have done studies to compare the cost of retaining a customer with the cost of gaining a new one. Most research reveals a difference of between 25 and 50 percent, which means that keeping a customer usually costs less than half the amount of bringing in a new one. Then why do so many businesses do such a poor job of customer relations? Because while management invariably tells its employees to focus on customer needs, it puts no plan in place to execute the strategy. "The friendly skies of United" are not always so friendly, and AT&T's long-distance information operators still act as if they don't want to be bothered.

One of my favorite stories from *In Search of Excellence** is about the two brothers who were going to be selling tickets at Walt Disney World in Orlando, Florida, during the summer months before returning to college in the fall. Their father was

*Tom Peters and Robert Waterman, Jr. (New York: Prentice-Hall, 1983).

amazed that Disney required them to spend four eight-hour days in training if all they were going to do was sell tickets, and for only a few months at that. The boys had to point out to their father that, unlike other companies, Disney had no employees; rather, workers were all members of "the cast." And Disney did not have customers as other businesses did; the people attending the amusement park were their "guests." It is true, the boys continued, that their primary function was to sell tickets, but some individuals might have wanted to know such things as the time the parade was to start or where the rest rooms were located. Considering that they were members of "the cast" and these people were their "guests," they told Dad, they had to know all these things. Isn't that beautiful?

Do your employees believe that they are members of "your cast," rather than employees, and that your customers are really "your guests"? If I were put in charge of a marketing team tomorrow, the first thing I would do is send everyone who interfaces with the company's "guests" to either Disneyland, just southeast of Los Angeles, or Walt Disney World. I wouldn't say a word. I would just let them soak up the customer relations on display. Walt Disney understood better than anyone in the world that customer relations is a critical part of marketing.

As discussed in Chapter 9, you have to be concerned not only with external marketing but with internal marketing as well. If you can successfully sell your business to your employees, as has been done at Disney and at Delta Airlines, it will be reflected in their dealings with your "guests." If you beat them over the head as was done by Frank Lorenzo, former CEO of Texas Air (now Continental Air), you may end up like these companies—in Chapter 11 bankruptcy.

To execute successful customer relations, the objective has to have management's top priority and the execution of the strategy has to be monitored. Management at many companies, including Coca-Cola and Procter & Gamble, periodically listen to taped telephone conversations between their employees and customers. What good does it do you to spend thousands of marketing dollars to obtain customers if you are subsequently going to lose them through faulty customer relations?

Section VI

Sales Management Plan

Managing the Sales Force

$\mathbb{S}$ales management is many things to many people, but for our purposes, the subject will be divided into three areas: planning, communicating, and training. This chapter covers the first two subjects, and the next chapter, the third.

Meeting the Sales Goals

The first planning priority is to detail where, how, and at what price sales will be made to meet the sales goals defined in the marketing objectives. Chapter 5 gave the reasons for including measurable objectives in the marketing plan. Measurable sales goals are also needed to establish an effective sales management program. Why? They provide regular feedback on results and increase motivation. They are an excellent basis for performance evaluation. They help achieve sales and profit targets and contribute directly to the accomplishment of companywide objectives.

These measurable sales objectives should not be set by management. Rather, as in management by objectives, salespeople should set their own objectives, subject to review by their superiors. Salespeople know the potential of their territories better than anyone else and should be given the opportunity to set their own performance standards. This does not mean that district or regional sales managers should not raise goals when they think they are set too low, but this should be done only after a discussion with the salesperson. The main point is that salespeople should be given the chance of developing their own goals and plans.

After the district and regional sales managers compile their sales forecasts, based on the data supplied by the salespeople, they in turn present the goals to the sales manager, vice-president of sales, or vice-president of marketing. Once again, there must be dialogue. Management may state that the figures are too low. If management insists on higher objectives, then the sales force may demand more sales personnel, more sales promotions, or more advertising. It is the dialogue that is important. Communication must be both upward and downward. The success of the plan depends on whether the people who have to execute the plan (the sales force) are of the belief that it is their plan.

At the time the sales objectives are set, and at frequent intervals thereafter, salespeople should have the opportunity to explain their own plans and programs to sales management. These plans and programs detail how the salespeople anticipate reaching their objectives. The plans don't necessarily have to be extensively documented. In fact, they don't even have to be written. The presentation could consist of a five-minute oral report followed by a brief question-and-answer period. If possible, other department heads should be present because these meetings are excellent opportunities to strengthen horizontal communication.

Performance review and evaluation is automatically accomplished at the regular meetings when salespeople make their reports. Strengths and weaknesses of individual salespeople are pinpointed, and it's easy to identify why they may be having a sales problem. Future action is clarified. This is not a checkup but an opportunity for salespeople to know where they stand and to keep score on their own performances and growth.

Sales Management by Objectives

This form of management, which could actually be called *sales management by objectives* (SMBO), is based on motivation programs of behavioral scientists, such as Herzberg, McGregor, Maslow, and Likert. Their programs emphasize that positive motivation is based on job content and the degree to which it enables personal growth, achievement, responsibility, and recognition—factors that satisfy the human need for constructive accomplishment. In SMBO, salespeople help plan and organize the program from the very beginning. They like this involvement by participation because it gives them recognition and a sense of accomplishment.

Supervision is also simplified in SMBO. Salespeople actually supervise themselves. Their personal plans for reaching important measurable objectives are clearly defined. Problems are identified in the reporting sessions. Between meetings, the sales manager can zero in on those areas where individuals need improvement. The meetings themselves are also of more interest. They are sharp and concise because discussion is concentrated on the salesperson's four to seven most important profit-making objectives. The usual long-winded speeches are eliminated because reports are condensed to five minutes. Interest is maintained because each salesperson is actively involved in his or her own job enrichment program.

Finally, accomplishment of goals becomes the basis for compensation under the SMBO plan. Good salespeople feel as if they are in business for themselves. Therefore, compensation based on measured accomplishment means more money in their pockets.

Sales management by objectives is not appropriate for all planning activities, but it can be applied to most. Other planning requirements include assessment of the strengths and weaknesses of your sales force and plans for sales force development; time management; individual market and customer planning to ensure a maximum return on each salesperson's efforts; analysis of the competition; analysis of current customers to obtain maximum sales volume from each; and plans for new product introductions, sales literature, conventions, trade shows, and so on.

Time management is a critical area that sales managers sometimes do not emphasize sufficiently to their sales forces. As mentioned earlier, in almost every industry, a small percentage of customers accounts for a very large percentage of total sales. The rule of thumb is 20 percent of customers are responsible for 80 percent of sales. In some businesses it is even more skewed. In car rentals, approximately 4 percent of the U.S. population account for 90 percent of total usage; 13 percent of the country consume 98 percent of the Scotch whiskey. Your people should ascertain who your heavy users are, then the next heaviest group, and so on. After this is done, they should determine which sales approach (and media weight) should be used for each segment. Personal visits may be programmed for the heaviest users, phone calls for the next heaviest, letters or mailed sales literature for the next, and then, possibly, no direct action for the remainder.

There should be little need this late in the book to re-emphasize the importance of planning. Managers at all levels, in all departments, have to set their objectives and then develop plans and programs to reach those objectives. Sales management has to determine its list of priorities to build a more efficient sales organization and then develop a planning program that will obtain the necessary results.

Improving Communications

Sales management by objectives can also solve many communications problems. In the SMBO reporting sessions, salespeople have the opportunity to explain to the group their activities, their problems, their successes, and practically any other information that they want to communicate. The frequency of these meetings depends on the location of the sales force. If salespeople are nearby, meetings should be held monthly. If a significant amount of travel time is required, meetings can be held quarterly. If salespeople are spread over a very wide area, meetings are usually arranged two or three times a year.

Between meetings, rather than having salespeople report the number of calls made, which is usually ineffective, consider some type of monthly progress report. In this type of reporting system, monthly and yearly sales figures, along with previously set objectives, are sent to salespeople based on their measurable objectives. The salespeople now have complete information regarding their operations and can make realistic accurate reports to management about why they are or are not on target. This is much better than making them fill out call reports on each presentation they make. Accountants have long emphasized the importance of "responsibility accounting." Instead of simply keeping records, a specific action is taken by each salesperson as a result of each monthly progress report.

15

Sales Training

Training requires both planning and communications skills. This chapter is devoted to a relatively new approach. The usual method of training new salespeople is by the watch-and-learn method. The new people are placed with experienced salespeople to observe the job until they have been trained. The big weakness here is that the new people usually learn the bad habits of the trainers right along with the good habits.

Any organization can be too rigid. In a short time, new employees can begin to look and act like everyone else. They may soon give up trying to sell their own ideas, approaches, and programs; they keep their eyes open and mouth shut and begin twenty years of payments on a retirement home.

The new approach, used successfully by many companies, permits the new salespeople to train themselves. First the job objectives are determined and carefully explained. A statement of job requirements that lists the things the new employees should know and be able to do in order to reach their measurable objectives is prepared. They are told of their responsibilities for training themselves and encouraged to communicate with anyone in the company. Then at regular intervals, the supervisor reviews and evaluates their progress.

The remaining pages outline a sales manual that uses this new approach. Rather than have new sales personnel learn from the existing staff, consider giving the new people a manual of this type and let them learn by themselves. You may be amazed at how many new, effective ideas they come up with on their own.

Requirements for an Effective Sales Presentation

Knowledge of your product or service is essential. However, what you say and how you say it is equally important. These thirteen guidelines tell what to do when you come face to face with everyday sales resistance. These commonsense communications principles also apply in every daily contact—on the job, at home, and in the community. They have been developed by working with hundreds of salespeople. Review them before starting every day's activities.

1. *Have a good ten-second opener.* First impressions are important. The first ten words of your sales talk are more important than the next hundred. Your opening sentence should get immediate attention, gain confidence, spark the entire presentation. It should create a favorable first impression—be arresting, stirring, and vivid. The use of one of the visuals you have available helps make a good opening.

2. *Emphasize what the product or service will do for the customer.* Customers are often more interested in what the product will do for them than they are in the mechanics. Sell benefits.

3. *Cover all important selling points on every call.* A survey on why salespeople lose sales indicated that in most cases it was because they did not tell a complete story. It is a mistake to assume that customers know and remember the sales points you have given them in the past. Make a written outline of the important points in your sales presentation. Although you may not always follow the outline exactly, it will enable you to include all the important selling points in each presentation.

4. *Proceed logically from one point to another.* Again, a written outline that has been fixed in your mind should help you. Tape-record your presentation. This will reveal repetition, poor sequence of ideas, "ahs," weak enunciation and voice modulation, and failure to tell the complete story. Your presentation should have continuity. Skillfully link all parts of the sales presentation together, and stay on the track.

5. *Anticipate objections and include them in your sales presentation.* For example, if your product or service sells at a higher price than the competition, explain the reasons for the higher

price and the key benefits. If your presentation is properly made, there will be few objections, if any.

6. *Use visuals to make a point.* The nerves of the eye are twenty-two times as strong as the nerves of the ear. Therefore, visuals are much more effective than when you merely explain your product. Surveys show that customers appreciate interesting, informative demonstrations. They get your sales points quicker and easier, and they remember them longer. Emphasis is taken off price and competition. Demonstrations add life, motion, interest, excitement, and showmanship to your entire sales presentation.

7. *Get the customer into the act.* Customers remember longer those parts of your sales talk in which they are allowed to do and say something. The desire to buy comes from letting the customer share the spotlight—to see and handle your product or visuals.

8. *Use "you," not "we."* Who is the most important person in the world to you? You are. If you were handed a new phone book, whose name would you look for first? Your own. If 200 people were asked to try out new pens, what would they write? Four out of five would write their own names. Yes, we all revolve around ourselves. Customers are interested in their own welfare and problems and in what savings and benefits you can offer them. Get on the same side of the fence as your customers.

9. *Check your progress in selling each benefit by asking questions.* For example, "You agree, Mr. Jones, that this would be a savings?" or "You can see how taking advantage of our complete service would save you money. Isn't that true, Mr. Jones?" Get the customer saying "yes" when you are closing the sale.

10. *Arouse curiosity.* When you were a child, you probably stood on the edge of the sidewalk and looked up at a tall building—and every passerby automatically followed suit. People are curious, and this plays an important part in everyday sales activity. If people weren't curious, few sales would be made. Some form of arousing curiosity can be used effectively in every presentation to get customers interested in and asking about your service. Place the product or visual demonstration

before the customer, and continue with your sales talk. When the customer's curiosity has reached a peak, hand the item to the customer and explain its features. Once you have your customer's undivided attention—the sale is off to a good start.

11. *How you handle your product, visual, or sales tool is as important as what you say about it.* Handle it with admiration. Dignify it. Enhance its value. Demonstrate, unwrapping your visual or product from a rich piece of cloth.

12. *Use a sixty-second close.* Summarize the key selling points, but close on the one that interests the customer the most.

13. *Ask for the sale.* My personal analysis of hundreds of sales talks shows that over 70 percent of salespeople fail to ask the customer to buy. Sales talks just trail off, and customers are left up in the air—without help that might make it easier for them to buy. Actually, the closing of the sale becomes easy if you have followed the preceding twelve guidelines.

If your sales presentation covers each of these principles, you are on your way to effective selling. Salespeople should present their talks to one another and grade each other on whether each principle is covered. Another method would be to tape yourself and then listen to be sure every point is handled adequately. But before you do this, read the remaining parts of this chapter, which provide additional input on preplanning calls, your first ten seconds, "people knowledge," benefits, organization, selling with a question mark, handling objections, and closing the sale.

Preplanning Calls

Do you just make calls, or does every call have a definite objective and plan? As a salesperson once told me, "On most calls I feel the sale is made or lost by what I do *before* the call." Another salesperson said, "I have so many customers with diverse problems that I'm forced to review the plan in advance in order to pick up where I left off on the last call."

These two statements point out the importance of planning each call in advance. Every call should have a definite objective and plan. Plans that do the trick aren't thought up on the spur of the moment.

Five points of information are needed to properly plan every call:

1. *If the customer is a new prospect, what is his or her business?* What do I know about the customer's needs and problems? Whether the customer is new or old, how can I and my product fill these needs and solve the problems? How can my program fit into the customer's overall operation?

2. *Whom should I see?* Am I calling on the person who has the authority to say yes? Can I get several people together at one time at a meeting?

3. *Where does the competition fit into the picture with this account?* If this is the competition's account, what can I offer over and above what the competition offers?

4. *What am I going to say?* I must be flexible to roll with the customer's remarks and desires. At the same time, I must tell a complete, not a hit-or-miss, sales story. Is my sales talk planned?

5. *What is the customer's credit rating?* With a brand-new account, this is important. Have I checked so as not to waste time on an account that can't pay for the products I sell?

Your First Ten Seconds

As stressed earlier, first impressions are important. A survey I conducted of over 200 salespeople indicates that less than 10 percent plan what they are going to say when they start their sales talks. Yet, the opener and its follow-up can be an important 50 percent of the entire presentation. Good openers are the result of careful study and thought and are not dreamed up on the spur of the moment.

Your customer's mind is not a vacuum. It's crowded with thoughts and problems, and you must compete with these. How long do you think you can hold the undivided attention of a customer or prospect? According to studies, you can do this for only a few seconds. Therefore, a good opener is required to set the stage for your complete sales talk by driving out all other thoughts from the customer's mind and opening it for your presentation.

Many salespeople find it easy to get immediate interest and attention by emphasizing customer needs, benefits, or a suggested solution to problems before they start talking about their product, their company, or themselves. A reference to the emotional needs a product or service will satisfy makes a good opener. Above all, your ten-second opener should be of direct personal interest to the customer.

Good sales openers indicate the possibility of:

- Solving one of the buyer's problems
- Saving the company's money or increasing its sales, thus making the buyer look better to the boss
- Raising the buyer's stature in the eyes of associates and the community; giving the buyer more job security
- Making the buyer's work easier—lessening worries and indirectly improving health

To obtain the information on which to base your first sentence, some preliminary study or diplomatic questioning is often necessary. A good opener is worded so the prospect will say, "That's interesting." It answers the question, "What's in it for me?" Effective openers can ask a question; use a gift, a referral, or a demonstration; arouse curiosity; or offer a service. "I'd like your opinion of . . ." is often used with new products.

Demonstrations, samples, booklets, testimonials, advertisements, catalog pages, and pictures have been used by successful salespeople in opening their sales talks. Curiosity can often be aroused to gain instant favorable attention by placing the sales visual or product in full view of the customer without comment. When curiosity has reached a peak, hand the item to the customer with an interest-creating sentence.

People Knowledge

Product knowledge is important, but effective selling takes "people knowledge," too! Authorities say at least half the art of selling is understanding the customer. Which is more important: You? Your product? Your customers? Most salespeople agree it's the customers. Yet in the hustle and bustle of everyday selling, we seldom stop to study the needs and desires that motivate them.

Human beings are often irrational and emotional. And more important, many purchases are emotionally influenced, especially when the product is similar to its competitors in quality and price. In other words, the heart is closer to the pocketbook than the mind is! That's why it is so important to consider the emotional appeals—the unconscious habits, purposes, desires, and motives that influence the customer's behavior.

Before each of your next calls, stop for a moment to consider your customers or prospects. Ask yourself these questions:

- How much do I know about the customers?
- What makes them tick? What do they want out of their jobs? Out of life?
- What are the things I can do for them? For their companies? And which of these things are likely to be most important today?
- Will my product make them more important to the boss? Will it give them more recognition in their departments? In the company? In the industry? In the community? In their families?
- Will it give them more security in the company? Can they sell my idea up the line?
- Will it take some of the effort and worry from their jobs and indirectly make them feel better and live longer?

For added sales insurance, build up an "emotional file" on each important customer and prospect. Diplomatically obtain your information from companies and friends outside the customer's business, from associates inside the company, and from observation and indirect questioning of the customer.

Add a Benefit to Every Product Feature

Features are special characteristics that make one product different from another. This includes what the product is; how it is made; how it is used; its history, appearance, merchandising plan, or service. Benefits are the end results—what the product will do for the customer. Customers don't usually buy products. They buy ideas—mental pictures of results, such as saving time or money, convenience, pride, prestige, less work and worry, or pleasure. Retailers look for products that will increase their sales and profits.

Your company manufactures products but sells benefits. One salesperson expressed it this way: "Don't only tell your customer how good you make your goods, tell him how good your goods make him." Unless the customer already has had some experience with the product, it is not safe to assume the customer knows the benefits of each product feature. What is quite obvious to the salesperson may not be so to the customer.

The more product knowledge salespeople have, the more careful they must be to slow down their sales talks enough to include a benefit at the end of each feature. Benefits and product features go together. Neither can stand alone. Both are necessary in every sales presentation.

Tell Your Sales Story in Logical Sequence

Have you listened to yourself lately? Have you checked your sales story to see that your customer benefits are told in logical sequence? Any rambling? Excess repetition? Is your sales story complete? And is it improving every month? Salespeople agree that the most popular, most interesting, and probably the best sales development aid ever created is the voice recorder (any tape or disc recording machine). Here's an example of how salespeople have used it effectively.

The salespeople of five companies in different fields all decided to analyze their presentations. They took several weeks to study their present talks, improve them, and check them with other salespeople and customers. The more ambitious read books on good selling techniques. Then each salesperson presented his or her sales talk into a voice recorder with another salesperson acting as the customer. A twenty-four-hour period was allowed to elapse before the salespeople played back and listened to their sales stories. This waiting period is essential in obtaining a true analysis of each presentation. Here is the salespeople's own summary of the most common weak points of their sales talks:

- Sales points not in logical sequence
- Too much rambling
- Excessive verbiage
- Too much needless repetition
- Too many "ahs" and "uh-huhs"
- Poor enunciation of certain words
- Grammatical errors
- No variety in voice pitch (voice modulation)
- Story not complete—a third to a half of customer benefits omitted
- Violations of the basic rules of selling

It is difficult to know exactly why or how, but the salespeople found that the voice recorder bared every weakness in their presentations. They could recognize their faults—immediately and clearly—and they could do something about them.

The salespeople then set about improving their sales presentations. They skillfully linked all parts of their presentations together into hard-hitting sales talks. They asked for suggestions from other salespeople and tried the talks on their customers. They continued to check and improve their presentations. The result was better and more concise sales talks.

The salespeople found it was often difficult to tell their sales stories in a planned sequence because of interruptions from the customer. These interruptions were often valuable indications of interest and needed to be capitalized on. The salespeople found the big advantage of the planned sales talks was that they could easily get back on the track and continue their stories in a logical, effective manner.

Is it ever wise to repeat important customer benefits? Most salespeople have found it helpful to briefly summarize all sales points just before the close, with special emphasis on the one benefit of greatest interest to the customer. One salesperson who took part in the above study had an interesting observation: "I have been selling for ten years. Have I had ten years of selling experience or one year of experience repeated ten times? The voice recorder gave me the answer."

Sell With a Question Mark

Get agreement on each idea before going on to the next. Salespeople admit that all too frequently they parade a number of selling points before the prospect without making certain the prospect is following them. They unload their entire sales story, trusting that the customer will be interested in some part of it and therefore will buy the product. Too much of the sales story gets lost this way.

A sales story is successful only when each benefit is completely understood by the customer. Prospects who fail to understand the presentation become indifferent. They may form false impressions, jump to conclusions, or even become irritated. One misunderstood sales point often breaks down the entire presentation. And remember, prospects are reluctant to admit they don't understand, until prompted by your questions. You know your products—but don't assume the prospect has the same knowledge.

The average person does not sustain attention for long periods of time. The mind wanders in and out of focus on what you are saying. People think faster than they talk and often let their minds wander when they should be listening. The average person talks at the rate of 150 words per minute but listens at the rate of 750 words per minute! This means that prospects have spare time to think about a number of other things while seeming to listen to us. They may be thinking about a pressing problem at home or at work. They may be preparing their next objections. It is important to focus their attention on each sales point—on everything you have to say.

Leading questions get customers to talk. They draw people out and center their minds on you and your product. Get customers saying "yes" throughout your sales talk, and they will be more likely to say "yes" when you ask them for orders.

Salespeople agree it is better to ask more leading questions and make fewer positive remarks. Questions usually create an impression of modesty and invite confidence. Too many emphatic statements may make the customer doubt your sincerity.

It is important to ask the right kind of questions—leading questions that get the answers you want; questions that get the customer talking and draw out any hidden objections.

A Thirteen-Step Plan for Disposing of Objections

1. Write out your best answers to all common objections.
2. See how other good salespeople answer the same objections.
3. Try your answers out on your customers. Which are the most effective?
4. Condense them into as few, powerful words as possible.
5. Rehearse them so the right answers flow out smoothly and naturally.
6. Anticipate objections by including most of the answers as positive points in your sales talk.
7. Continue to recheck and improve answers.

When a prospect brings up an objection:

8. Relax. Don't interrupt. Don't be overanxious. Sit back in your chair, but remain alert and businesslike.
9. Listen. Let the prospect talk it out. An objection that's bottled up builds up. Whenever you let a person blow off steam, the objection seems less important. Often prospects will realize this and may even answer their objections themselves. In the meantime, you are gathering important facts—you are getting the objection out in the open.
10. Don't disagree. Your prospect expects you to disagree, and if you do, your are begging for an argument. For example say, "I understand how you feel about this problem." Then continue with a question.
11. Question. Make sure you understand exactly what the prospect means. You can say, "I wonder if you'd tell me more about it," or "I'm not quite sure I have the complete picture. Can you give me more details?"
12. Qualify. To make certain you have smoked out the real objection, you can say, "Then the real point that's bothering you is. . . ."
13. Capitalize. Now that you have pinned down the key objection, you can answer it intelligently.

Close the Sale

Be sure to close the sale. As mentioned earlier, the majority of salespeople never ask the customer to buy. The sales talks just trail off, and customers are left up in the air.

The use of reassurance just before you get ready to try for the close is one of the shrewdest forms of salesmanship, because all buyers on the verge of spending money need to be reassured that they are acting wisely and in their own best interests. Be sure to establish credibility with the buyers— credibility in yourself and in the benefits of the product or service.

Usually you should close as soon as you can and not allow any sales talk to drag on longer than necessary. Even if you have not presented your complete talk, if you get any hints that a close is at hand, drop everything, stop talking, step in, and try to close. Regardless of the situation, this rule still holds.

The following are seven closing techniques that you should be familiar with so that you can apply them smoothly in your sales presentations.

1. *Assumption.* In this approach, you take it for granted that the prospect is going to say "yes." Salesman Frank Better used this technique over and over again on his way to becoming a millionaire.

2. *Secondary question.* In this approach, you ask the prospect a simple question, and a response, in effect, approves the sale. Normally, you word the question so that the reply cannot be "no." For example, "Do you want delivery on the twentieth or the thirtieth?" "Do you prefer the product in gray or in black?" "Do you prefer the large or the medium size?"

3. *Physical act.* Here you do something that the buyer will have to stop to avoid giving tacit approval to the purchase. It is safe to say that nine out of ten sales should be closed with this approach. You can ask the buyer to use his phone to check a delivery date. One salesperson rolls a fountain pen toward the buyer; unless the buyer picks up the pen to sign the purchase order, the pen will fall on the floor. Another salesperson gives

the buyer the order blank to sign, then takes it back to check it over again, and finally gives it back to the buyer to sign.

4. *Immediacy.* In this case, you inform the buyer that if the item is not purchased now, it will cost considerably more because of inflation, increase in cost of goods, and so on. As the story goes, if someone were to come into my house at three o'clock in the morning, wake me up, and tell me that by going downstairs I would make $100, I would kick him down the stairs and go back to bed. But if the same man were to wake me and tell me that by getting up and going with him I could avoid the loss of $100, I'd say, "Just wait till I get my pants on."

5. *The third party.* For some reason, we all have a great deal of interest in the opinion of other people. Furthermore, we would believe what a user of a product or service says much more readily than we'd believe the person who makes it or sells it.

One sales manager, rather than having his salespeople put their testimonial letters in a neatly bound kit, insists that they carry as many as possible in their inside suit pockets. This enables the salesperson to take one out at a time and lay it on the prospect's desk. As soon as the prospect has glanced at one, the salesperson brings out another, and so on and so on, until the prospect's desk is literally covered with testimonial letters.

6. *Special inducement.* Everybody likes a bargain, and if you are in a position to offer the prospect something additional for signing now, then this approach can be a very effective closing.

7. *Ask for the order.* As one salesperson states, "I ask the customer for the order at the earliest possible moment. If he says 'yes,' I'm in luck. If he says 'no,' he uses fifty words to explain, and I get a tip on what is going through his mind. Having found out what he is thinking about, I continue my story until I can again ask for the order. The prospect either says 'yes' or gives me another 'no.' If his reply is 'no,' he has to think up another fifty words to explain."

Section VII

The Complete Marketing Plan

16

Pulling the Marketing Plan Together

The marketing plan consists of objectives, strategies, and plans that cover the proposed activity planned within each of the five previously discussed marketing components. For each component, such as the sales plan, you should have three to five measurable objectives. An objectives signifies what you want to accomplish. It has to be measurable; otherwise you will not know whether you have accomplished what was planned. To be measurable, you usually need three parts: a goal, a control, and a date. Increasing the sales closure rate by 10 percent and increasing awareness from 30 percent to 50 percent are examples of goals. However, if you don't add a control, perhaps a limit on spending, you can reach your goal but bankrupt the business. A control could be an expenditure of $50,000, for example. And you need a date by which the goal should be achieved: by December 31, 19XX.

Figures 16-1 to 16-7 contain a recommended marketing plan format. In this format are examples of objectives for each of the five components of marketing. The goals are stated within their respective sections, and the controls and completion dates are discussed in the final section (Figure 16-7), on budgets, timing, and action plans.

For each objective, you need one or more strategies. The strategies delineate how you plan to accomplish the objective. Then you need one or more plans detailing how you will execute each strategy. In the marketing plan, you summarize the plan and put the details in separate action plans.

Your marketing plan should be the operational plan that runs your marketing team. Because it is operational, it has to be referred to each week. If you prepare a marketing plan and then put it on the shelf for twelve months, save yourself the time of preparing it; it's just an exercise. If you find you are off target, the plan has to be changed. If an objective is not being met, you have to change either the objective, the strategy, or the plan. If you wait until the end of the planning year, you have lost a lot of time.

In addition, your marketing plan, if prepared correctly, should become the job descriptions of all members of marketing. That means all job descriptions that have existed in time more than one year should be thrown out. Each time the marketing plan is changed, the job descriptions are altered.

The marketing plan and resulting job descriptions should also set the structure for bonuses and advancement within the company. Those individuals and departments that make or exceed the measurable objectives set forth in the plan should be the ones rewarded.

Figure 16-1 contains a recommended outline for a marketing plan and its first section. The strategic position is a summary of your strategic plan for this particular market, as discussed in Chapter 1. The marketing personnel section should list the components of the company included in the plan, the personnel involved (including an advertising agency if applicable), and the marketing team planning leader, as discussed in Chapters 2 and 3.

The fact book summary is an overview of your findings concerning the market, the competition, the customer, and your own operation, as discussed in Chapter 4. The complete fact book, which should be extensive and which, if done correctly, usually runs from 100 to 200 pages, should be kept separate from the marketing plan. Otherwise, you will have a marketing plan so thick no one will ever read it. When you present your plan, bring your fact book with you, but only summarize it in your presentation and then go immediately into your plan. If someone questions a decision made in the plan, refer to your fact book.

The major objectives and strategies inserted in this first section are the ones you believe most critical to the success of the plan and usually encompass more than one of the five components of marketing. Various subjects to be considered are listed in the figure.

Figures 16-2 through 16-6 are devoted to the objectives, strategies, and plans for each of the five components of marketing. Each one contains hypothetical examples.

Figure 16-2 is the place for your objectives, strategies, and plans for your own product or service, as discussed in Chapter 5. Figure 16-3 calls for your objectives, strategies, and plans for your advertising plan, sales promotion plan, and public relations plan. (These subjects were discussed in Chapter 6 through Chapter 10.)

Figure 16-4 requires your objectives, strategies, and plans for your research plan, as discussed in Chapters 11 and 12. Figure 16-5 should contain your objectives, strategies, and plans for your customer service activities, as discussed in Chapter 13.

Figure 16-6 contains your objectives, strategies, and plans for your sales management program, as discussed in Chapters 14 and 15.

You don't need the last section, shown in Figure 16-7, if you decide to put the information shown here in the preceding sections. This section calls for your goals, controls, and dates. You can either put all three requirements of your objectives in their respective sections or use this format, inserting your goals in their respective sections and then listing all your controls (budgets) and dates (timing) in the last section of your plan. The subject of actions plans have been added to this last section to remind you to get your marketing plan approved first before they are completed.

Figure 16-1. Marketing plan format: Outline and Section I.

OUTLINE

Section I: Strategic Position, Marketing Personnel, Fact Book Summary, and Major Marketing Objectives and Strategies
Section II: Product/Service Plan
Section III: Marketing Communications Plan
Section IV: Research Plan
Section V: Customer Service Plan
Section VI: Sales Management Plan
Section VII: Budget, Timing, Plans, and Action Plans

Section I

Strategic Position, Marketing Personnel, Fact Book Summary, and Major Marketing Objectives and Strategies

A. Strategic Position

   1. Relative profit potential of this market within the company. Example: a new market with the highest profit potential of all markets in which the business is currently competing.
   2. Critique on company versus competition as to current status as well as ability to acquire the critical business strengths needed to become major player in this market.
   3. Definition of strategic position and payout. Example: Strategic position will be to go for maximum market share and become market leader with a break-even in five years.

B. Marketing Personnel

   1. State which components of the business are involved in the marketing function.
   2. If you employ an advertising agency, state its role in the preparation of the plan.
   3. State the name of the planning leader for the plan, the members of the planning team, the individual who is responsible for keeping the fact book up to date, and the individuals responsible for monitoring the various sections of the plan to be sure the strategies are executed correctly and the objectives are met.

C. Fact Book Summary

   1. Statement on marketing aspects of the market.
   2. Statement on marketing strength of competition.

   3. Definition of target audience.
   4. Delineation of company marketing strengths and weaknesses for competing in this market.

D. Major Marketing Objectives

   1. Market share objectives.
   2. Distribution and depth of line objectives.
   3. New product/service introduction objectives.
   4. Awareness, preference, and sales closure rate objectives.
   5. Repeat purchase rate and volume/profit per purchase objectives.
   6. Marketing budget and timing.
   7. Gross sales, gross margin, operating margin, and net profit objectives (sum of all functional plans: R&D, engineering, manufacturing, operations, marketing, and G&A).
   8. Return-on-investment (ROI), return-on-assets (ROA), return-on-net-assets (RONA), and/or discounted cash flow (DCF) objectives (sum of all functional plans).

E. Major Marketing Strategies

   1. Positioning statement. Example: Position the brand in the segment of the market of consumers who desire more preprogrammed options, thus extending the use and value of the brand. This target is the numbers-oriented person (e.g., the engineer, aviator, accountant, or retailer).
   2. Distribution strategy. Example: Position the brand among dealers as the most attractive service to the above-mentioned target, one that is not currently being reached by brands Able and Baker and thus not a duplication of inventory. Develop in-store merchandising units to demonstrate and allow consumer to "work" new model, thereby reinforcing brand difference at point of sale.
   3. Communications strategy. Example: Thrust of marketing communications will be consumer "pull" rather than dealer "push." Build brand awareness and recognition of brand difference with target consumer, first through specialized media and later through mass media.
   4. Pricing strategy. Example: Price competitively with major competition.

Figure 16-2. Marketing plan format: Section II.

Section II

Product/Service Plan

A. Product/Service Plan Objectives

   1. Set objectives for subjects such as allocation of marketing dollars per product/service, distribution, depth of line, packaging, pricing, awareness, preference, and repeat purchasing.

   2. Examples:

      a. Model 1040 and 1041 will receive 90 percent of marketing dollars due to higher profit margins.

      b. Increase the average price to $1,961 on models 1040 and 1041.

      c. Expand distribution among chains from 29 percent to 50 percent, among department stores from 50 percent to 75 percent, and among independents from 17 percent to 35 percent.

      d. Reduce packaging costs to $2.50 for chains, $2.25 for department stores, $1.50 for owned and operateds (O/O), and $3.00 for independents.

B. Product/Service Plan Strategies

   1. Set one or more strategies for each objective.

   2. Examples

      a. All advertising and sales promotion will feature models 1040 and 1041. In addition, sales force will receive double bonus points on these two models.

      b. Prices will be raised for O/Os and independents to $2,100, coupled with the company's pledge for greater advertising support. Chain and department stores pricing will remain the same.

      c. Major expansion in distribution will be obtained through a 35 percent increase in the sales force and a 25 percent increase in the communications budget.

      d. The new technology on vacuum packaging developed last year by R&D will be used for all models within the next two years.

C. Product/Service Plans

   1. Develop at least one plan for each above strategy. The plan states how you plan to execute the strategy.
   2. Summarize the plan in the marketing plan and put the details in action plans. The action plan should include each step or task, who is responsible for each step or task, and the date by which each step or task has to be completed. If the strategy is to use trade shows to accomplish a certain objective, then the action plan should delineate each step necessary to execute the strategy, including selecting the shows, booking the space, designing the exhibit, and determining who will attend.

Figure 16-3. Marketing plan format: Section III.

Section III

Marketing Communications Plan

A. Marketing Communications Plan Objectives

   1. Include objectives on advertising, sales promotion, and public relations.

   2. Advertising Plan Examples

     a. Among senior data processing professionals in companies with sales over $20 million, increase awareness of Ryan minicomputer from 30 percent to 50 percent. Increase association with major selling point (more data storage per dollar) from 25 percent to 40 percent.

     b. Among dealers of small computer systems, increase awareness of brand from 25 percent to 45 percent and association with major selling point from 15 percent to 30 percent.

   3. Sales Promotion Plan Examples

     a. Demonstrate high-impact resistance of new housing on energy monitors to 300 design engineers.

     b. Reduce sales time necessary to educate purchasing agents on specifications of thermocoupler line from an average of ninety minutes to thirty minutes.

     c. Generate $50,000 in direct sales of replacement parts.

     d. Reduce the number of unqualified leads sent to the sales force by 50 percent.

   4. Public Relations Plan Examples:

     a. Placement of two major articles in general business or weekly news magazines.

     b. Placement of major article on new Series 100 line in every data processing publication.

B. Marketing Communications Plan Strategies

   1. Set one or more strategies for each above objective.

   2. Advertising Plan Examples:

     a. Creative Strategy

       (1) Major benefit: more data storage per dollar.

       (2) Copy points: Competitively priced; offers twice the num-

ber of circuits per chip; supports 30 percent more sectors per track versus competition.

  b. Media Strategy

    (1) Reach 65 percent of senior data processing professionals in companies with sales over $20 million with a frequency of eight over a twelve-month period.

    (2) Concentrate all media dollars in the leading trade vertical magazine, adding second magazine in the field only if necessary to reach required reach.

3. Sales Promotion Plan Examples

  a. To demonstrate impact resistance of new housing, take space in July WESPLEX show and design exhibit offering prize to anyone cracking housing with sledge hammer. Publicize exhibit and prize by direct mail to design engineers.

  b. Review brochures on thermocoupler line to incorporate complete specifications and clear explanation of differences between each item in the line.

  c. To build direct sales program for replacement parts, start with list of customers with models three to five years old. Set up system of twenty-four-hour handling of orders. Create approach to stress this fast service, resulting in less downtime for customer.

4. Public Relations Plan Examples

  a. Use lure of exclusive sneak preview of Series 100 line and/or set up exclusive interview with CEO for major business/newsweekly article.

  b. Fly in editors of all data processing publications for preview of Series 100 three months before introduction in order to secure major coverage in their May editions.

Figure 16-4. Marketing plan format: Section IV.

Section IV

Research Plan

A. Research Plan Objectives

    1. Set objectives for methods you will use to measure: the effectiveness of your marketing plan; changes in the market and new product/service development.

    2. Examples

        a. Conduct a statistically projectable study of the target audience to obtain current levels on awareness, registration of selling message, preference, and intent to buy.

        b. Determine needs of the company's customers and the current ranking of the company's customer service department concerning the competition.

        c. Determine two leading benefits of new model 707 to the aircraft instrumentation industry.

B. Research Plan Strategies

    1. Set one or more objective for each of your strategies.

    2. Examples

        a. Conduct a benchmark study of 300 members of the target audience with a standard deviation of 2 and a precision of plus or minus 3 to obtain effectiveness levels on marketing communciations.

        b. Have an independent company conduct a free seminar on customer service for marketing personnel of current and potential customers; during the seminar, elicit from the customers their own needs and their current observations on performance of their suppliers, including our company.

        c. Conduct six focus group sessions among purchasing agents in aviation instrumentation companies as a guide to determining major benefits of model 707.

Figure 16-5. Marketing plan format: Section V.

Section V

Customer Service Plan

A. Customer Service Plan Objectives

  1. Set objectives for the performance of customer service (e.g., effectiveness ranking within the industry, management involvement, marketing involvement, knowledge of product/service line, number of telephone rings before response, cost of handling returns, and expertise of technical personnel).

  2. Examples

    a. Company will be ranked number one in the industry in customer service effectiveness within two years.

    b. All phones will be answered by the third ring.

    c. Customer service personnel will have access to all marketing information available to product managers.

B. Customer Service Plan Strategies

  1. Set one or more strategies for each objective.

  2. Examples

    a. All customer service personnel will be given a free weekend trip to either Disneyland or Disney World to permit them to observe the finest customer service organization in the world.

    b. An independent company will be commissioned to answer any customer service phone after two rings. The customer service department will be charged the complete cost, which will be deducted from customer service employees' bonuses.

    c. All customer service personnel responsible for product/service knowledge will have access to a computer database that will allow them to punch in a few numbers to bring up on the computer monitor any type of information on any product/service sold by the company.

Figure 16-6. Marketing plan format: Section VI.

Section VI

Sales Management Plan

A. Sales Management Plan Objectives

   1. Set objectives on subjects such as sales goals per product/ service line, sales closure rate, cost per sales call, number of sales calls per day, and sales training.

   2. Examples

     a. Maintain current field force of twenty people on service A and increase sales from $910,113 to $995,000.

     b. Increase average sales closure rate from current 22 percent to 28 percent.

     c. Average 20 percent of sales force calls by field force on service B to frequent travelers to speed up penetration of this market.

     d. Increase division profitability by increasing sales of service C from 30 percent to 35 percent.

B. Sales Management Plan Strategies

   1. Set one or more strategies for each objective.

   2. Examples

     a. Improve field sales force productivity on service A through a combination of efforts including: forming home office unit with 1-800 telephone number lines to take over customer tracking and routine reorders and creating series of direct-mail pieces to qualify inquiries before sending to field.

     b. To increase closure rate, a minimum of one-third of the entire sale force will be sent to a new one-week session on sales training that will incorporate a new concept of "town meeting" dialogue to improve each individual's ability to close.

     c. To increase penetration of service C, hire ten new salespeople to work as task force rolling out service as each new region is targeted.

     d. To increase proportion of sales of service C, create bonus compensation plan based on points awarded according to margins on various services.

Figure 16-7. Marketing plan format: Section VII.

Section VII

Budgets, Timing, Plans, and Action Plans

A. Budgets

All objectives should be measurable to enable you to determine whether you meet them. That means they usually require a goal, a control, and timing or date. In the preceding pages there are several examples of objectives with goals. You can put the control (usually the amount of money to be spent) or the budget in each objective, or you can put the control for each objective in summary form at the end of the plan.

After you have approved goals and controls, monitor them each week to be sure you are on target. If you are off target sometime during the year, you have to change either the goal or the control or alter the strategy.

B. Timing

Timing refers to the completion by which the objective must be achieved. Like controls, the timing can be inserted in each objective or can be summarized at the end of the plan. Like controls, timing has to be continuously monitored.

C. Plans

Plans are the execution of the strategies. They should be summarized in the marketing plan. After the complete marketing plan is approved, action plans should be written to provide the details. If you include all the details of executing a strategy in the marketing plan, you may be confronted with three possible problems:

1. You end up with a 50- to 200-page document that no one will read, and the plan just gathers dust on the shelf.
2. If the plan is not approved, you have wasted time developing all the details.
3. Using a separate action plan lets the people who will actually execute the plan decide for themselves how they should do it.

D. Action Plans

An action plan contains the detailed execution of one or more strategies and should include at least three factors:

(continues)

Figure 16-7. Continued.

---

1. Each necessary step or task
2. Who will be responsible for accomplishing each step or task
3. The required completion date of each step or task

For each marketing plan, you may have between five and twenty action plans. The sum of all your action plans is your milestone calendar or perk chart. A milestone calendar keeps you on target relative to timing. A perk chart determines which completion dates for certain steps or tasks are the most critical and have to be watched most closely. These critical steps or tasks are the ones that influence the beginning of another step or task.

Keep your action plans in separate documents. Your fact book should also be in a separate binder. This will enable you to have a short, concise, operational marketing plan that you can refer to each week. If your marketing plan is not operational, the preparation is nothing more than an exercise.

Conclusion

$\mathbb{B}$ecause you have now been given a considerable amount of information, it may be beneficial in this last chapter to provide you with a brief summary of how to execute the contents of this book.

Everything starts with strategic planning. This sets the direction of your business. In which markets should you be trying to gain market share? Which products should be positioned for share maintenance? Which ones should be phased out? The sum of the approved strategic plans becomes your corporate objectives and determines the type of marketing plan to be employed in each market.

The document that contains all the information you need to know about the market, the customer, the competition, and your own business in order to develop an intelligent strategic plan is called a situation analysis. The document that is primarily marketing oriented but that covers the same four subjects is called a fact book. You prepare the fact book before you start on your marketing plan; a complete fact book should ensure a sound marketing plan, whereas an incomplete fact book probably ensures an ineffective plan.

After the fact book is completed, you select a representative of each marketing function (sales plan, marketing communication plan, customer service plan, research plan, and product/service plan) to serve as a member of the planning team and present the fact book. Then, as a group, you develop your plan. If a representative has a problem within her area, she goes back to her department, solves the problem, and reports back to the group.

After the plan is completed, it is presented to management by the planning team leader. Upon approval, it becomes the operational plan of the marketing function, and the measurable objectives of the plan become the job descriptions of the marketing team. Their future with the company should depend on their ability to reach their objectives.

However, the plan has to be monitored weekly. If a particular objective is not on target, either the objective, the strategy, or the plan has to be altered. Marketing is not a science; therefore, you will never write the perfect plan. However, it is the companies that watch the reactions to their plans and then make adjustments that come out on top.

It's time to tee up the ball.

Index